THE NEW REGIONAL AGENDA

Edited by Jo Dungey and Ines Newman

A joint publication of the Local Government Information Unit
and the South East Economic Development Strategy

CONTENTS

PREFACE 5
Richard Caborn MP, Minister for the Regions, Regeneration and Planning

SUMMARY AND SUMMARY OF RECOMMENDATIONS 7

INTRODUCTION 17
Ines Newman and Jo Dungey

1 REGIONAL STRATEGIES FOR THE 29
KNOWLEDGE ECONOMY
Michael Ward

2 THE ECONOMIC ROLE AND FUNCTION OF RDAs 37
Ines Newman

3 THE IMPLICATIONS OF RDAs FOR URBAN POLICY 51
AND SUB-REGIONAL PARTNERSHIPS
Stuart Wilks-Heeg

4 RDAs AND EUROPE 59
Adrian Colwell

5 REGIONAL CHAMBERS: THE EXAMPLE 69
OF YORKSHIRE AND HUMBERSIDE
Liz Kerry

6 THE WEST MIDLANDS: TAKING FORWARD 77
THE REGIONAL AGENDA
Andrew Coulson

7 THE ENGLISH REGIONS AND THE WIDER 85
CONSTITUTIONAL AND ADMINISTRATIVE REFORMS
John Mawson

8 FROM REGIONAL DEVELOPMENT 99
TO REGIONAL DEVOLUTION
Alan Whitehead MP

REFERENCES 106

ABOUT THE CONTRIBUTORS 108

The Regional Development Agencies Act opens up exciting new opportunities for the regions. The purpose of the Agencies is to address the economic deficit in England's regions. In doing so they will be concerned not just with business competitiveness but also with issues of social exclusion, regeneration, skills and training, and sustainability, all of which contribute to the regions' economic performance.

Regional Development Agencies have caught the mood of the times. People want regional solutions to regional problems. The strategies which RDAs develop will be developed in close partnership with all the regional players. Successful RDAs will raise the profile of the English regions and make it possible for more regional initiatives to take root and bloom.

Local authorities are key agents in this new agenda. They have the local knowledge of needs and opportunities which will be a vital element in regional strategies. They also have the ability to support and galvanise other partners; and they are directly responsible for a wide range of local services relevant to regional economic performance. In recognition of this we have appointed four members of local authorities to the Board of each RDA. Their experience and knowledge will be invaluable in cementing links between local and regional agendas.

Local authorities are also leading the creation of regional chambers which will support and scrutinise the work of RDAs. Chambers may also increasingly take on other regional roles extending beyond the RDAs' economic development remit. RDA chairs have welcomed the contribution which chambers can make to ensuring that RDAs respond fully to the concerns of the whole of their regions.

I therefore welcome this timely publication which clearly identifies what action local authorities and other agencies should take now to contribute to RDAs' developing regional strategies. These strategies will build on regional strengths and address the weaknesses which have held back economic performance in the past.

I hope that local authorities will read this publication carefully and act on its recommendations.

Richard Caborn MP,
Minister for the Regions, Regeneration and Planning

Introduction

The introduction sets out some background to the government's decision to create Regional Development Agencies for England. The main roles of the RDAs are to develop an economic strategy for the region and ensure it is implemented; to develop strategies for skills and innovation; to take responsibility for regeneration, including the regeneration of rural areas, and to market the region as a business location. Other areas of regional policy are being strengthened, including planning guidance, transport policy, industrial and skills strategies, and cultural policies. These developments have major implications for local government who will wish to influence them, particularly through the regional chambers.

Section 1: Regional strategies for the knowledge economy

This section sets out an overview of the main characteristics of the successful regional economy of the future. In the face of globalisation and technological change, the growth area for the future is 'the knowledge economy': design, research, product development, education and the professions. The task of the RDA should be to set out strategies based on a rigorous analysis of the strengths and weaknesses of the current regional economy, and to foster development of new sectors. This requires strong international links, enhanced research and development capability, good transport infrastructure, and high levels of educational achievement. RDAs must also tackle social exclusion and develop strategies to integrate the long-term unemployed.

Section 2: The economic role and function of RDAs

RDAs were originally envisaged (Regional Policy Commission, 1996) as the powerful executive agencies of democratically accountable regional bodies. However, they have been created as Non-Departmental Public Bodies, and many government programmes central to economic development remain with the DTI and DfEE. The legislation does allow for RDAs to evolve and be given additional functions, and local authorities will need to consider what these additional functions should be. The initial role of RDAs is primarily concerned with strategy development, partnership building and regeneration. RDAs must work to integrate economic growth, social inclusion and sustainability. The RDA must work within a complex institutional framework, and local authorities will need to be clear about the relative roles of agencies within the economic development agenda.

The involvement of RDAs in partnership and strategy development will make it complex to monitor outcomes of their work. However, frameworks will need to be established to monitor the achievements of the RDAs. Local authorities, through the chambers, will have a vital role in this and will need to agree a clear understanding of what outcomes they expect the RDAs to deliver, and establish arrangements for monitoring them.

Section 3: The implications of Regional Development Agencies for urban policy and sub-regional partnerships

Urban policy and regeneration are evolving a new consensus around improved integration of mainstream services and the need to locate specific local regeneration within a wider regional economic context. Other important principles for the future include development of public-private partnerships, the need to balance physical and social regeneration, and to develop cross-departmental and cross-sectoral working.

The RDAs will take over allocation of the Single Regeneration Budget. It remains to be seen whether this will lead to an evolution away from small area regeneration approaches towards more regional and strategic uses. There is already interest in making regeneration more effective by linking it to a wider regional strategy to be set by the RDA. However, there is concern that a move away from small area regeneration could result in the neglect of more community oriented approaches. The creation of RDAs is also likely to strengthen the importance of partnership working at a local, sub-regional and regional level. Local government and the new chambers will need to ensure that there is adequate openness and accountability, and that overlapping and conflicting partnership agendas are integrated into coherent strategies.

Section 4: Regional Development Agencies and Europe

Involvement with the European Union, particularly the structural funds, has been an important influence in encouraging local government to think more about regional economic strategies.

The RDAs will have a significant role in relation to the European Union structural funds. The structural funds are being revised for the period 2000-2006, with regional competitiveness as a central theme. Once the new regulations are negotiated, the EU will require comprehensive regional economic development strategies as a framework for implementation of the new programmes. It is vital these strategies are integrated with RDA objectives. RDAs will need to establish close working relationships with other partners involved in the structural fund programmes, which will cover the same regional areas.

RDAs and chambers will also be affected by other areas of EU policy, including: the EU's strengthened commitment to environmental impact assessment; the reform of the Common Agricultural Policy and moves to establish comprehensive rural development policies; changes affecting Assisted Area status; and implications of the National Employment Action Programmes. The likely expansion of the EU in Central and Eastern Europe will give new possibilities of involvement in programmes with these countries. The fact that MEPs will be elected on regional boundaries will also impact on their role in the new regional agenda.

Sections 5 and 6: the Case Studies

In the English regions there are a range of existing regional groupings, which are evolving rapidly into bodies which can work with Regional Development Agencies. Two examples are described:

Section 5: Regional chambers: the example of Yorkshire and Humberside

The Regional Assembly for Yorkshire and Humberside brought together the work of three pre-existing structures: the Regional Planning Conference; the Yorkshire and Humberside Regional

Association; and the European Office. It is a strategic body working to create a co-ordinated programme linked to the work of a wide range of agencies. The partner organisations have been through a process of review of strategies to develop a shared vision for the region, published as *Advancing Together*. This outlines five strategic objectives: an advanced economy; robust infrastructure; sustainable environments; a skilled and flexible workforce; and enhanced quality of life for all. There is a commitment from the partner organisations to work to achieve this. The Regional Assembly has also entered into policy debates, which will affect the region, such as the reform of the EU structural funds and the Common Agricultural Policy. The Assembly has evolved into a regional chamber, which will seek designation under RDA legislation.

Section 6: The West Midlands: taking forward the regional agenda

The West Midlands has developed a strong regional local government association, with representation of all councils in the region. This body has structures which deal with a wide range of social and economic issues on a regional basis. It has taken over responsibility for Regional Planning Guidance. This local authority body is likely to continue alongside the regional chamber, which will include business and other representation. There is a range of views about how the present structures will evolve with the establishment of the RDAs. The immediate task is for local authorities to work with the RDA to maximise the potential benefits for their region.

Section 7: The English regions and the wider constitutional and administrative reforms

The establishment of RDAs and chambers needs to be seen in the context of the wider constitutional changes taking place in Britain, such as the establishment of new Scottish, Welsh and Northern Ireland bodies. These bodies will create new relationships with local government in their areas, and also provide new opportunities to tackle the role of quangos in public provision.

The new Greater London Authority will provide an alternative model of accountability with the London Development Agency.

These developments will create a need to ensure coherence between the different elements of the government's devolution policies. There is potential for greater conflict over matters such as geographical allocation of public funding, and competition for assisted area status or inward investment. There is a range of options for central government to respond to these challenges. This could include developing improved regional working in all government departments, Executive Agencies and quangos; improved information on the regional distribution of public spending, and improving the mechanisms for managing the links between the parts of the UK. There is a potential new role for the Government Offices for the Regions in ensuring co-ordination within the English regions, and providing an access point to government, but this will require changes in the Whitehall machinery.

Local authorities will have to develop their capacity to work within the new regional framework, but they will have access to new avenues of influence over other areas of public provision in their regions.

Section 8: From regional development to regional devolution

Taking a longer term view of where the government's devolution policy is heading, it is acknowledged that there are a range of views and ambitions within local government about the future of regional structures and regional government. However it is argued that there are constitutional benefits for local government in the successful establishment of a regional tier in England. If local government wants to see further progress on decentralisation and devolution, RDAs and chambers need to succeed. Greater London is a particularly interesting model of the relation between an elected authority and regional development agency. Local authorities need to contribute to the debate on how regional bodies could move to direct election and on appropriate regional boundaries in the longer term.

Summary of Recommendations

This publication emphasises the evolving nature of the regional agenda. However the authors emphasise that there is much local authorities and other agencies can do *now* to ensure effective, locally accountable and responsive structures emerge at the regional levels. It is also essential that local authorities clarify their view of how they would like the agenda to evolve in the longer term and lobby for appropriate change. Below we summarise the key recommendations of the report in terms of immediate and long term recommendations.

More detailed recommendations appear at the end of each section.

What local authorities and other local agencies should do now

Developing the chamber and its role in relation to RDAs

In order to maximise their influence over regional strategies, local authorities need to contribute to the success of regional chambers. This includes:

- supporting members who are on chambers, and on RDA boards
- allocating the necessary time and resources to regional work
- clarifying the role of chambers both in relation to RDAs and as a wider partnership body
- ensuring local communities are consulted and that their capacity is developed and they have the appropriate support to be involved in new regional strategies
- making local authority experience of public/private partnership formation available to RDAs with a particular focus on disseminating models of best practice
- considering how the wider European agenda could be addressed in the regional partnership in which the RDA will be involved.

Contributing to RDA strategy

Local authorities will have their own economic development expertise to contribute to regional economic strategy. They will also, in partnership with other stakeholders in the chamber, and other bodies in the region, need to contribute to analysis, information and strategy development. To do this they need to:

- ensure that regeneration and economic development does not become too narrowly focused on economic growth, but integrates issues of sustainability and social exclusion and inequality
- use existing powers, experience and activities to influence RDA strategy. These include regional strategies developed by the chamber; powers in relation to spatial planning, including Regional Planning Guidance; an integrated transport strategy; and partnership building
- start work on new European regional strategies now. Ensure that strategies developed by the chamber and RDA are linked to strategies and programmes under the European Union structural funds.
- continue to mobilise community-based sub-regional and regional partnerships so that local authorities are in a stronger position to express collectively their views on the allocation of SRB resources.
- develop their contribution to regional economic strategies, and their own role in the implementation of such strategies.

Monitoring and supporting the RDA

Local authorities will need to support the role of the RDAs, and also, through the chambers, agree arrangements to monitor their work. This will include:

- developing a clear understanding of the nature of the economic development function they expect from RDAs.
- agreeing appropriate indicators
- agreeing baseline data

- scrutiny and review of the allocation of resources
- drawing together reports on the activities of RDAs, which state if their impact and added value is in line with aims not only of economic development, but also issues such as social exclusion, equal opportunities and sustainability
- monitoring of RDA achievements, which will need to be co-ordinated with evaluation required by the European Union structural fund programmes.

It is essential that there are clear agreements about subsidiarity – to ensure that RDAs are defining and working only on clearly regional issues, and that local strategies are the responsibility of local government.

Longer-term regional structures

Many commentators do not see the present structures as stable in the longer term. Only central government can resolve that, but local authorities will be concerned to have a strategic, cohesive approach to constitutional reform. Local authorities therefore need to lobby for:

- mechanisms to co-ordinate the work of all departments, Executive Agencies and quangos with the new regional working, and regions with Whitehall
- a clear and powerful entry point for Government Offices for the Regions into the Whitehall machinery of government
- the development of a clearer institutional structure at local and regional level in the economic development field, especially in the area of training and business support functions, with defined institutional responsibilities and less overlap
- development of the relationships between the new structures of the British nations and regions, to reach agreement on resource allocation and co-operation.

In additional, local authorities need to address the issue of what development of regional structures they want in the longer term. In doing this:

- the development of the relationship between the Greater London Authority and the London Development Agency should be closely monitored as a possible paradigm of future chamber/RDA relations
- the prerequisites of a move to directly elected regional bodies need to be considered, including whether local government wishes to endorse a test of support for regional assemblies by way of a rolling endorsement by local authorities, rather than a one-off referendum. Also to be decided is whether there should be linkage with a move to unitary local government
- local government should consider whether it supports mechanisms to be in place providing for the formation of regional assemblies on boundaries other than those of the current Government Offices for the Regions.

The government's new agenda for the English regions provides a major challenge for local government, and for other agencies at a local level. In this publication we clarify the issues and provide a guide to action.

Eight different experts have provided summaries on aspects of the government's regional policy, the implications of this, and where they think we should be going.

The Regional Development Agencies Act is a new step in the rapidly changing constitutional and economic development framework. Few commentators see the current situation as a stable one, but as the contributors to this publication emphasise, the new agenda provides opportunities that local agencies need to grasp *now*, both to get the best out of the present arrangements and to influence how the framework will develop in the future.

Background to the new regional agenda

First, some background. The establishment of Regional Development Agencies brings together aspects of the new government's economic and constitutional policy.

The constitutional agenda for the English regions was laid out in 1995 by Jack Straw in the consultation document *A Choice for England* (Labour party, 1995). This paper proposed a strategic authority for London and regional assemblies on the same boundaries as the integrated Government Offices for the Regions. However, these assemblies were to be created only after successful referenda. In the meantime voluntary regional chambers would co-ordinate economic and other strategies.

The new Labour government also had commitments to a Scottish parliament, a Welsh Assembly, and a new Greater London Authority if referenda supported them, and to a new Assembly in Northern Ireland, as part of a wider agenda of constitutional change. This constitutional agenda was linked to a regional economic agenda.

The Ministers now responsible for regional economic policy in government – John Prescott (Secretary of State for the Environment, Transport and the Regions) and Richard Caborn (Minister for the Regions, Regeneration and Planning) – both have long track records of concern about the uneven economic performance of the different regions. In opposition, John Prescott encouraged the establishment of the Millan Commission, to look at this issue. The Commission's report *Renewing the Regions* is a key document in understanding the background to the RDAs.

The main recommendation of the Millan Commission was that "...RDAs be established, separate from the regional chambers, but responsible to the chambers and acting as their executive arm in the area of economic development." (Regional Policy Commission, 1996).

After the general election in May 1997, it became clear that Prescott and his colleagues were only going to be given time for one simple parliamentary bill on English regions and that there was considerable opposition within the cabinet to radical regional devolution. The constitutional reform necessary for paving the way for assemblies was dropped for the lifetime of this parliament. The Regional Development Agencies Act was put forward, establishing quangos responsible to central government, with voluntary chambers being encouraged but given a consultative/advisory role in relation to RDAs. But it was made clear that the RDA act was an "enabling" act that would facilitate the devolution of more central government powers and the reorganisation of the numerous organisations involved in economic development over time. This is the context in which this publication is written.

The case for change in the English regions

Advocates of regional devolution have pointed to the need for institutions with an incentive to tackle England's long-term regional economic disparities, and with the ability to develop new and more appropriate economic development initiatives. Experience of working with the European Union structural funds has highlighted the case for regional economic strategies, and drawn attention to the existence of regional democratic structures in other European countries. The emergence of European "spatial planning" concepts linking planning, environmental, transport and economic agendas has also helped to make the case for regional institutions which can develop an appropriate policy framework.

The campaigns for Scottish and Welsh devolution have been seen as creating a need for 'balance', with some parallel decentralisation in England. Devolution to allow regional policy co-ordination and delivery and democratising existing regional structures have all been seen as increasingly important.

However, for a range of reasons, devolution to the English regions was a less clear-cut option than the establishment of a Scottish parliament. Support for regional government among the public in England was clearly not at the level of support for some form of Scottish body. In Scotland there had been years of campaigning, culminating in the Scottish Constitutional Convention, as well as a substantial block of public support for independence. Nor could Scotland, which has had a separate legal system and other separate institutions since the Act of Union (and before), provide a model for the English regions.

Among the barriers to regional government in England we could include:

- the continuing two tier system of local government in much of England and the legacy of conflict from the previous government's attempts to reorganise local government
- uncertainty about public support for new structures, especially if they could be presented as an additional tier of government/bureaucracy
- the varying levels of regional identity in England
- disputes about regional boundaries, in some cases reflecting political and other intra-regional conflicts.

The pressures towards further regionalisation are likely to dominate. This is evident in the two case studies in this publication and in the contributions from John Mawson and Alan Whitehead. There may be resentment from English regions with more powerful neighbours in Scotland, Wales and London. The European agenda continues to focus on regional strategies.

The government's own emphasis on joined-up thinking will necessitate the development of a regional dimension. The new voluntary regional chambers will seek to consolidate their role.

Finally, the sections on economic development by Michael Ward and Ines Newman indicate that the economic agenda will bring its own logic to bear on the range of powers of chambers and RDAs.

Establishing the RDAs

The Chairs of the RDAs (other than London) were announced in August 1998. The RDA Act completed its passage in November 1998. The boards were appointed in December. The Secretary of State has published guidance on regional chambers and RDA strategy. RDA offices are being established, bringing together personnel from GORs, English Partnerships, the Rural Development Commission, Regional Development Organisations, and often with secondees from local government. The RDAs will be fully operational from 1 April 1999.

London

The development agency for London will be accountable to the new Mayor. The Greater London Authority, consisting of a Mayor and Assembly, will be elected in May 2000. In the interim period, there are shadow arrangements run by the London Development Partnership.

WHAT THE ACT COVERS

The Act establishes Regional Development Agencies covering all the English regions – nine, including Greater London. The boundaries of RDAs are to be those of the current Government Offices for the Regions, other than that Merseyside will be part of the North West region.

Role of Regional Development Agencies

The legislation defines the purposes of an RDA as being:

- to further the economic development and the regeneration of its area
- to promote business efficiency, investment and competitiveness in its area
- to promote employment in its area
- to enhance the development and application of skills relevant to employment in its area, and
- to contribute to the achievement of sustainable development in the United Kingdom where it is relevant to its area to do so.

Key roles of the RDAs include:

- development of an economic strategy for the region, and oversight of its implementation
- developing a regional skills agenda and regional innovation strategy
- responsibility for regeneration, including the administration of the Single Regeneration Budget, taking over regional functions from English Partnerships, and "a leading role" on European structural funds
- development and regeneration of rural areas, including taking over functions from the Regional Development Commission
- marketing of the region as a business location.

The White Paper also described RDAs as contributing to policies on transport and land use planning, further and higher education, crime prevention, housing, public health, tourism, culture, and sports.

Functions and staff are to be transferred from English Partnerships, the Rural Development Commission, and the GOR.

Many existing agencies will continue their current functions, including TECs. Business Links, and some other economic development functions will remain with the Department of Trade and Industry. However, the Act allows Ministers to transfer government functions to the RDAs, either (with consent) to specific RDAs, or to all of them. This means that RDAs, if seen to be a success, could acquire a broader role without new primary legislation.

RDA structure

The RDAs are Non-Departmental Public Bodies (quangos) appointed by the Secretary of State for the Environment, Transport and the Regions, and accountable through the Minister to Parliament. They will be scrutinised by the Public Accounts Committee and the National Audit Office.

The new agencies are to have boards of twelve (the Act says the boards must have between 8 and 15 members), including about half their members drawn from businesses, four from councils, and others from other sectors.

Role of regional chambers

The legislation allows the Secretary of State to designate appropriate bodies as regional chambers. The chamber will provide a means of local and regional consultation and accountability.

Both the legislation, and guidance from Ministers define the criteria for regional chambers. The chambers are required to have majority local authority representation, with some representation from all the main political parties. They should also include a wide range of non-local authority representatives (no less than 30 per cent of the chamber), from the main regional stakeholders. No partner should be excluded from membership because of funding requirements.

The RDAs will be under a duty to consult regional chambers. The Secretary of State can issue guidance and direction about the role of the chamber and other consultation. The RDA would be required to have regard to the regional viewpoint of the chamber in preparing its own economic strategy, and be open to scrutiny by the chamber.

Financial provisions

The Secretary of State has the power in the Act to direct an RDA to repay to the government any part or all of any surplus held by the RDA. RDAs will be able to borrow up to £200m externally subject to the approval of the Secretary of State and Treasury.

Scope of the legislation

The Act gives scope for further powers to be given to RDAs without need for further primary legislation. It does not however enable chambers to develop into directly elected regional bodies. It is very unlikely that this will become possible within the current parliament. Chambers may well want to have a more pivotal role than outlined in the legislation and will be making their case for this.

OTHER ASPECTS OF GOVERNMENT REGIONAL POLICY

There are a range of other ways in which the government is strengthening its regional policy.

Regional Planning Guidance

Regional Planning Guidance is currently developed by regional planning conferences of local authorities, for approval by the Minister. With the establishment of the RDAs, their economic strategies will have to integrate with the Regional Planning Guidance. Similarly, Regional Planning Guidance will need to take note of the RDA's strategies.

The government is keen to avoid legislation in the short term, so is adopting a system where formal responsibility for RPG would remain with the Secretary of State but responsibility for the preparation and content would rest very largely with the relevant regional planning conference working in partnership with the GOR. New guidance has recently been issued on public examinations. The Regional Planning Guidance is also to present a strengthened integrated transport strategy, and include the spatial aspects of environmental and economic policy.

This will strengthen the powers of regional local authority bodies over issues of importance to the RDA, such as: land use, including industrial and commercial locations; the currently controversial issue of new housing land; and transport and other major infrastructure issues. Regional planning policy provides an additional vehicle for leverage over regional economic strategies for local government.

Transport

Regional Planning Guidance is also to incorporate the new integrated transport strategies. These are to be drawn up in close consultation with the relevant regional chamber, and also involve the strategic Rail Authority, the Government Office for the Region and the Highways Agency. Thus the RPG will incorporate public transport issues; guidance on off-street parking in new developments; strategy on the role of airports and ports in the region; regional priorities for transport investment; traffic management issues which require regional consideration; and guidance on road charging and parking levies. The regional transport strategies need to take account of RDA strategy.

Trade and Industry

The Government Offices for the Regions have issued competitiveness strategies for 1998-2008 and some have established Competitiveness Forums. The Department of Trade and Industry has developed regional competitiveness indicators (February 1998) and these are now being regularly monitored. It is unlikely that the regional competitiveness strategies will be updated before the establishment of the RDA and they will probably subsumed into the RDA economic strategies. This will require close working between the RDA and GOR which retains control over the majority of DTI powers.

Skills strategy

The government has issued a consultative paper on *TECs: Meeting the Challenge of the Millennium* (DfEE, 1998). The current structure is that the Government Offices for the Regions develop a skills strategy and contract with the TECs. The RDAs will take over responsibility for developing the skills strategy but contracting will remain with the GORs until the review of TECs is completed and the RDAs have had time to find their feet. There is still a major debate about the future role of TECs and their relationship with the RDAs (see Michael Dorsmen 1998, and Plummer and Zipfel 1998).

Cultural policy

The Department of Culture, Media and Sport produced proposals in August 1998 to create stronger regional co-ordination in the areas of their responsibility. The Department is to be represented in GORs from April 1999. Cultural activity, sport and tourism are seen as having an important role in social and economic regeneration.

The department propose to bring diverse funding bodies together into more powerful cultural groupings in each region. As well as a strengthened Regional Cultural Forum, an executive body would have a funding role including lottery, working alongside RDAs and regional chambers. A regional cultural strategy is proposed for the issues with which DCMS is concerned.

This could provide a regional dimension to the emphasis the government has put on the economic importance of the cultural sector. Tourism, sport, film, records, television, publishing, design, advertising, new media, and so on are seen as potential British strengths, and as vital industries of the future.

Health

Advocates of regional government have been interested in developing a stronger regional role within the health service. Concern exists about the lack of a local democratic input to health service decisions, and a regional rather than a local role in decision-making and scrutiny may be more appropriate.

However, health does not feature in the government's current regional priorities. Although the NHS Executive does have regional offices, these are not all on the same boundaries as the Government Offices for the Region, and the Department of Health has not been represented in the GORs.

Alongside issues of the administration of the NHS, the government has also shown determination to tackle causes of ill-health such as poor diet, poverty, and poor housing (for example in the White Paper *Our Healthier Nation* (Department of Health, 1998)). It may be that a regional, as well as a local, agenda will develop around these issues, tied to the concern to tackle social exclusion.

Regional institutions and the relationships between them

In most regions there are now four key regional institutions. It will be vital for a region's success that the relationship between these four institutions is clearly understood by all those involved. All the contributions focus on this issue, while the two case studies in particular highlight ways forward. In summary:

- **The Local Authority Association or Assembly:** This body varies from the Regional Assembly for Yorkshire and Humberside to the West Midlands LGA. In several cases the local authority body responsible for developing Regional Planning Guidance, the Regional Planning Conference, has been integrated as a sub committee into an LGA or Assembly structure, strengthening local authority partnership working. In the South East this is more complicated as the SERPLAN boundaries do not reflect the Government Office boundaries. So there remain overlapping local authority bodies – the South East Regional Forum, the Eastern Region Conference, the new Greater London Authority and SERPLAN (the planning body for the whole of the South East including London) and SCEALA (the Standing Conference of East Anglian Local Authorities: the planning conference).

  Whether one or more organisations, these local authority bodies have the function of developing Regional Planning Guidance for submission to the Secretary of State, and form a focus for developing and representing the local government view at regional level.

- **RDAs:** RDAs will be private sector led and their key function will be developing and delivering regional economic development strategies including regeneration. They will have a consultative role in relation to a series of other strategies – such as planning, environmental and transport strategies.

- **Regional chambers:** Regional chambers will become the key partnership organisation in a region. They will be local-authority-led but will deal with the holistic joined-up thinking agenda. As Liz Kerry says in her description of Yorkshire and Humberside: "the Chamber is about trying to get consensus about what the region needs to do in a whole range of areas, recognising the linkages between them and then ensuring delivery". This implies a wide range of stakeholders, including representation from community, voluntary, environmental, rural, social, welfare, health, transport, cultural, community safety, and education organisations – as well the economic actors. In this context there are already difficulties in fitting into the small 30 person chamber advocated in government guidelines, particularly in the larger regions. Representation, ways of working, accountability and empowering the community and voluntary sector will continue to be issues for chambers.

The Regional Development Agencies Act gives the chambers the right to be consulted by the RDA, within the terms of guidance issued by the Secretary of State.

● **Government Offices for the Region:** John Mawson's contribution clarifies the important role of Government Offices for the Regions. They have the potential to act as the single clear voice of Whitehall in the regions and to provide a clear and powerful entry point into the Whitehall machinery of government. Significant reform of Whitehall and a more transparent and open way of working in the GORs will be necessary.

All the contributions emphasise the importance of developing a clear understanding of the role and functions of these regional institutions and how they will work together.

How does this affect local government?

Some of the strongest advocates of elected regional bodies for England come from local government. However, from others in local government there is considerable scepticism. Local government is likely to want regional bodies to involve real decentralisation from Whitehall, and not take powers from the local level.

However, there are many problems caused for local government by unemployment and other economic disadvantage. Despite much work by local government on economic development, many fundamental problems cannot be tackled solely at a local level. So local government is likely to want to influence RDAs and to see them succeed. Our contributors look at the implications for local government and make recommendations for action.

Regional Strategies for the Knowledge Economy

Michael Ward
Director, Centre For Local Economic Strategies

Regional Policy: the new global context

The new Regional Development Agencies have the potential to become the most imaginative and ambitious initiative in regional policy since the first development of policies on the location of industry in Britain in the 1940s.

Rightly, the new emphasis is on the development of indigenous regional economies. Rightly, because we no longer live in the post-war world in which the original regional policy could flourish. National governments can no longer move companies around like pieces on a chessboard.

In part, this is because the geography of economic unevenness has become far more complicated. All regions now have pockets of unemployment and disadvantage: even London and the South East benefit from European regional funds as well as national government assistance. Of course, the older industrial regions still bear the brunt of unemployment: but a simple set of south/north transfers is no longer sufficient.

Second, however, and more important, companies are no longer organised on a national basis. Firms no longer choose between locations in the South East of England and locations in the North East. Instead, their choices will include lower labour-cost areas, within and beyond Europe, and sub-contracting to companies in the emerging economies.

In an unprecedented period of change, the old patterns of industrial location have been swept away. As well as globalisation, there is technological and managerial change: dispensing with layers of traditional jobs, and enabling companies to source components, processes, or product wherever in the world is most advantageous.

THE NEW REGIONAL AGENDA

The changing nature of work

Work itself is changing. The old distinction between manufacturing and services is no longer enough to describe the reality of the British economy. Routine jobs, whether traditionally classified as blue collar or white collar, manufacturing or services, have been disappearing: they are the most vulnerable to the new international competition and to technological change. Assembly-line work in factories, and clerical jobs in the finance sector and in insurance, have been equally vulnerable. In each case, the core elements of such jobs are routine, repetitive work. Often, such jobs were men's jobs, but, especially in offices, some traditional areas of women's employment have gone as well. Regional economies that traditionally depended on such jobs now have to reinvent themselves: communities where traditionally people built motorcars, or railway equipment, or made textiles have had to find a new role as these industries are restructured across Europe and beyond.

A second category of jobs, with quite different characteristics, are those in personal services. Personal service jobs - everything from school meals to hair-dressing, from street cleaning to childcare – are not disappearing. Personal service jobs occur in both the public and private sector: in an area like home care for elderly people, for example, there is both a market sector (for people able to hire help individually) and a public sector (a home-help service, rationed according to need).

Such jobs are vulnerable neither to technological change nor to globalisation. Their numbers are either static or growing. But, typically, these jobs do not offer the best wages or conditions in a local economy: 'real' jobs they certainly are, but they do not compensate those who have lost traditional employment.

The key jobs for regions in the future are a third group: the knowledge economy jobs: jobs in design, jobs in research, jobs in product development, jobs in teaching, or work involving a professional skill. Typically, they are jobs that require information technology skills, and higher education qualifications. It is those jobs in the knowledge economy that are crucial for prosperous regions.

Integrated strategies

The regional economies that the new Regional Development Agencies will inherit in April 1999, therefore, have changed and continue to change. In these circumstances, the old strategies – development of serviced sites and buildings, campaigns to attract foreign direct investment, venture capital funds, and the provision of infrastructure – will not be sufficient. Instead, these policy instruments will only function as part of an integrated regional strategy, designed to identify the key elements of change in the future, and be part of a process of 'reinventing' the regions.

The knowledge economy

A first element of such a regional strategy must be to build the knowledge economy. It is clear that those knowledge economy jobs flourish best in certain conditions. Regions need dynamic higher education institutions, with a reputation for excellence, and good links to business and entrepreneurs. They need well-developed business services – a strong presence by banks, and the professional firms that aid and support companies in developing. They need good international transport links: the new geography of Europe will be dominated by those regions with direct daily air services to Brussels, Paris, Frankfurt and other key European commercial centres. Regions need a strong cultural infrastructure.

These are the key factors of building a strong labour market for knowledge economy jobs: a labour market in which people with the new skills are not tied to a small handful of employers, but have a choice of a range of private and public sector organisations, as well as information technology companies themselves.

In his book *The Work of Nations,* the American economist Robert Reich (Reich, 1991) refers to knowledge economy jobs as "symbolic analyst" jobs and identifies "symbolic analyst zones" – the areas where people working in the knowledge economy choose to make their homes. These may be urban, rural or semi-rural areas: Islington, the Cotswolds, or the Cheshire Plain. But building the clusters of such jobs is critical.

In this context, the RDAs will need to address the existing tensions between rural and urban areas: the key concentrations of higher education, business services, and educational and cultural facilities are almost always to be found grouped in and around the major cities and regional capitals. But the economic links between those cities and their hinterlands are of critical importance.

Internationalisation

Second, successful regional economies of the future will be international: their businesses involved in an international division of labour, with access to international markets. In part, this comes back to effective international communication, airports and high-speed rail services. One indicator of the internationalisation of a regional economy is the extent which it has direct air services with European, North American and Far Eastern destinations.

Another indicator is the presence of international companies. This should not be seen solely in terms of inward investment projects creating large manufacturing plants. Certain parts of the country, in particular the North East and Wales, have succeeded in attracting major new plants in this way. But the overall analysis of change in the world economy suggests that such investment, although welcome when it comes, may not stay very long; and recent experience in 1998, with decisions by both Siemens and Fujitsu to close major manufacturing plants in the North East of England underlines how vulnerable such projects can be.

The major measure of the internationalisation of a region and its economy is the extent of the presence of European, North American and Asia-Pacific companies. Such a presence will not always – or normally – be a large manufacturing plant: it may be a small team, exploring sales, research, development, opportunities, or looking for partners for joint ventures. The Japanese management writer, Kenichi Ohmae has commented that, all over the world, civic leaders have asked him how they can get a major Japanese manufacturing plant: they never ask how they can get a research plant, although establishing new research capacity, especially where it builds on indigenous resources in the higher education sector, may be a far more effective way of developing the potential of a region. Regional strategies will need to identify the conditions in which such new investments by international companies can flourish: the evidence of existing foreign direct investment programmes is that regional clusters can be beneficial. Another indicator of internationalisation is the extent to which regions succeed in attracting international or European institutions. London has its fair share of international bodies: other British cities have few. Yet Lyon has Europol, and Strasbourg the European parliament.

Linking investment policy to skills

A third characteristic of an effective regional strategy needs to be the integration of investment policy with labour market policy.

The emphasis of traditional regional policy was on incentives, loans, and grants: the package designed to cajole the footloose company into locating within the region – or, occasionally, to persuade the home grown company to stay. But in the future, the effective area for public intervention will be as much skills and labour market policy as investment policy. For a knowledge economy company to expand and grow in a region, they need to know that there will be a continuing supply of people with the necessary levels of educational achievement. Therefore, the agencies will need to concern themselves, not only with the activities of TECs and training providers (And, sooner or later, the logic for incorporating TECs within the RDA structure is likely to become overwhelming.), but also with the formal education process in schools, and further and higher education.

It is no longer realistic for people to expect to acquire a skill before the age of 25 and to use it throughout their working lives. Companies will increasingly require flexible, educated people, ready to retrain, and to acquire new skills, on several occasions within their working lives.

Joining up the social and the economic

Fourth, the regional strategies must challenge head-on the traditional dichotomy between economic and social policy. There is a new agenda, one of combating social exclusion: a recognition that those marginalised by economic change, thrown out of traditional employment and concentrated into deprived communities, should not be simply be the subject of welfare or maintenance programmes, but should be actively helped back into the labour market. This new employment-centred, social policy is a major challenge to the new RDAs: their strategies must address the question of ensuring that new jobs and investment benefit those who have lost out in earlier rounds of restructuring.

Especially with younger people, education is of critical importance: anybody who has the potential to find work in the new knowledge-based industries needs support in acquiring the skills to do so.

However, in the areas of high unemployment (the disadvantaged neighbourhoods pinpointed by the recent report of the Social Exclusion Unit (SEU, 1998)) other solutions will be required as well. There is now a body of experience, using not-for-profit, 'social economy' organisation to create real, waged jobs, designed to integrate long-term unemployed people back into the labour market. The 1993 EC Delors White Paper on Growth, Competitiveness, and Employment (Commission of the European Community, 1993) pinpointed service areas – local transport, childcare, support for elderly people, and environmental work – as providing key opportunities for this type of job creation.

Sustainability

The White Paper setting out the proposals for Regional Development Agencies emphasised that they must integrate environmental sustainability into their strategies. The recent Transport White Paper (DETR, 1998) provides a framework for doing this: too often, in traditional structure plans and economic development strategies, sustainability has been relegated to the position of an apologetic afterthought, rather than a central element of the strategy.

Beyond land use planning

RDAs will have an important role in relation to strategic guidance under the land use planning system. But if their overall strategic role is to meet the new challenges, then the strategy process must be led by a clear, informed analysis of the state of the regional economy – of trends within it, and of measures to boost the knowledge economy – to stimulate internationalisation, to integrate investment and labour market policy, to bring social and economic objectives together, and to integrate sustainability into the whole, rather than being driven by physical investment projects. There will be a place for investment in infrastructure: but it must be led by the overall analysis. That overall analysis must be sufficiently rigorous and well researched so as to command a consensus among the partner organisations and the regional chamber. It would be a very welcome change if RDAs could, collectively, adopt a self-denying ordinance: while they will all engage in strong advocacy of the region, from time to time some sober analysis, which gives a realistic account of prospects, acknowledging problems as well as strengths, would be helpful.

Implications for local government

The emergence of RDAs, taking a broad, holistic view of their strategic responsibilities, will be a major challenge for local authorities. Local authorities, through the regional chambers, will have an input: they will not have the final or decisive say in strategy. Councils themselves have learned to work with the same range of partner organisations as will join them in the RDAs. But the new approach to strategy, bringing together social, economic and environmental policy, will demand that councils, too, review all their policies. It is by now commonplace to say that policies of central and local government – entered into for the best of intentions – have contributed to the growth, rather than the elimination, of social exclusion. Councils will need to look at the whole range of policy: education, housing, cultural and arts policy included, to ensure that these support and encourage the growth of the knowledge economy, and the integration of social and economic objectives.

Local government, too, will need to be ready to join with central government and other partners in a serious review of who does what in economic development. With the institution of the RDAs, there are now too many players: RDAs, TECs, local authorities, Business Links, *ad hoc* local partnerships and other bodies – none with a secure revenue base, none with a distinct set of statutory functions, all competing for the same limited sums of government money. Local authorities, as the democratic representatives of their communities, have a central role in regeneration: responding to economic change is one of the most important challenges facing civic leaders. But it will be in the interests of all the partner organisations to establish a clear division of labour between the different players.

RECOMMENDATIONS

- RDAs need a clear, informed analysis both of the state of the regional economy and of measures to boost the knowledge economy, linking social and economic objectives and integrating sustainability into the whole
- Councils need to re-examine the whole range of their existing policies to ensure that these support and encourage the growth of the knowledge economy, and the integration of social and economic objectives
- Local government needs to join with central government and other partners in a review which clarifies the roles of the different agencies involved in economic regeneration.

The Economic Role and Function of RDAs

Ines Newman,
Co-ordinator, South East Economic Development Strategy

Ines Newman,
Co-ordinator, South East Economic Development Strategy

TWO

Will Hutton argued in his book *The State We're In* (Hutton, 1995) that the successful economics of the future will be those which can provide the infrastructure, investment and human resources which allow industrial clusters to develop. These cannot be provided by central government but require powerful flexible, regional agencies which are responsive to local business needs and locally accountable.

This is very much the vision that has informed RDAs, and is reflected by Richard Caborn: "…only when we devolve down to the regions the framework and decision-making necessary to enable each to maximise its strengths, to build up core, world-class industrial and technological networks in each region, with the training and skills to match, can we hope for a step on the up-escalator to prosperity." (Murphy and Caborn, 1995).

The RDA's role is therefore seen as being that of a key economic development agency which can dramatically improve the economic performance of the region. The ability to achieve this vision, in the government's view, required a powerful executive agency, responsive to local business needs, and therefore private sector led. But the way the RDAs have evolved in practice raises a series of issues around their ability to achieve this vision and their local accountability in trying to succeed. This section seeks to clarify the key economic development issues; to draw out what this means for local authorities; and finally to identify what local authorities should be expecting from RDAs and how they can monitor their actions.

Issues

Understanding Competitiveness

Competitiveness has been defined by the government as "the ability to achieve sustained improvement in net output for a business; in Gross Domestic Product (GDP) per head for a region. It means doing what is necessary to meet the demands of today, whilst building the capability to improve performance compared to other businesses and regions in the future" (DTI, 1995). The problem is that it is not clear what constitutes the "capability to improve performance".

In the past most government resources to support businesses in the regions has come through Regional Selective Assistance and support for inward investment. Significantly the inward investment functions of the DTI are the only ones that are being devolved to RDAs.

However, while recognising the benefits of foreign direct investment, the government has increasingly realised that there is a need to shift the balance of industrial assistance towards support for a range of factors that are said to affect competitiveness, such as education, communications and infrastructure, research and development, skills enhancement, embeddedness, and so on (see the DTI White Paper *Competitiveness: Forging Ahead* (DTI, 1995)). There is also the realisation that a firm's competitiveness does not necessarily lead to equal benefits for the whole community and a more bottom-up approach is required in disadvantaged communities.

But this agenda is very complex (Dunning, Bannerman and Lundan, 1998). Many of the policies aimed at creating the conditions for competitiveness (for example, encouragement and support for research and technological development and innovation; and increasing the skills of the workforce) are long-term measures and their impact on productivity, particularly in the short term, is hard to measure. Changes in macro economic conditions (for example, the strong pound) can have a dramatic impact on competitiveness and destroy any productivity gains that have been made. This will all make it very difficult for an RDA to show it has achieved the government's vision and it will lead to the spending priorities of the RDA budget being contested. Finally the implementation of the programmes in these areas remains the province of the DTI and DfEE. This raises the possibility that RDAs will fall back on prioritising financial support for capital investment through their inward investment and English Partnership functions, despite the fact that the theory on which they are based emphasises networked and learning economies.

Conflicting Objectives: Competitiveness, Inclusion and Sustainability

Given the nature of the RDAs, as private-sector-dominated 'quangos' with a focus on strategy formulation, it is important that they reflect the wider political objectives of the government rather than narrow business interests. It was for this reason that Richard Caborn has said that he gave them responsibility for the SRB budgets – this puts social exclusion at the centre of their programmes. In addition, the purposes of the RDAs, as set out in the Act, include the promotion of employment and contribution to the achievement of sustainable development in the UK. In the long term, competitiveness will be threatened if part of the workforce is socially excluded and unable to develop the necessary skills to meet growth demands. Similarly economic development that threatens the quality of life or that uses resources in an unsustainable way will also threaten long-term competitiveness. The problem is that in the short term these objectives can conflict sharply.

While we can hope that partnership approaches lead to synergy and a win-win situation, there is the danger that RDAs will divert public resources away from meeting social needs and towards support for unsustainable projects through a focus on inward investment and profile building.

Institutional Issues

An Executive Agency? – The rationale for small, private sector RDAs rests on the ability of such agencies to enter complex, confidential negotiations and take quick, decisive actions. The RDAs were originally seen as the executive arm of regional chambers that would be responsible for the economic strategies (Regional Policy Commission 1996). Now, however, they have been given responsibility for the economic strategy itself but the power over specific programmes within the strategy rests with other agencies: the GORs and DTI for Regional Selective Assistance, supply chains, SMART innovative programme, and so on; TECs for training and skills development; Business Links for business support; the Higher Education Funding Council for university funding and Further Education Funding Council for further education funding.

In addition the RDA has been given a consultative role in the development of a series of other strategies, most recently the regional integrated transport strategy. It is clear that RDAs could get bogged down in partnership building and commenting on policy development – a role for which local authority bodies are far better suited because they carry legitimacy and can more easily develop trust relations.

On the other hand RDAs may be weak on the delivery of those actions which are associated with high rates of regional economic innovation and growth.

Monitoring Achievement – With the lack of clarity around the actions required to achieve competitiveness; the nature of competitiveness itself; and the relationship of competitiveness to sustainability and social inclusion, it will be extremely complex to monitor the success of RDAs in terms of economic development. Yet local authorities will need to develop a clear scrutiny role.

An Evolving Institution Framework – Ministers have made it clear that they expect RDAs to take on additional functions. There is also continuing devolution to GORs and the hope that, one day (but not in this parliament), there will be a firmer statutory basis for regional chambers and assemblies, and Regional Planning Guidance. This poses an issue for the emerging voluntary regional chambers and local authorities as to how far they lobby to increase the powers of RDAs in the economic development field and how they see the role of GORs and regional chambers in economic development.

What do these issues mean for local government?

Setting the Framework

Emerging regional chambers are seeing their roles as integrating Regional Planning Guidance, the new integrated regional transport plans, development of environmental, and Local Agenda 21 strategies, and the RDA's economic strategy. Several regional associations/emerging chambers are also starting to put together an economic strategy or statement, effectively pre-empting the work of the RDA in this area. Local authorities do have a clear role in defining the key objectives and framework for a regional economic strategy which should meet the triple aims of competitiveness, sustainability and inclusion, and should deal with how conflicts between these priorities should be resolved.

Clarifying their understanding of the RDA's role in economic development

If the four local authority members on the RDA are to be effective a common understanding of the RDA's role needs to be developed. It would be helpful for local authorities and emerging regional chambers to go through the following list and clarify under each issue: first, what they expect the RDA to do; second, the emerging chamber's role; and third, the role of the local authority.

Research and Strategy Functions – RDAs will have a key role in developing regional economic intelligence. The purpose of such intelligence needs to be specified so that it is collected in a useful way. For example, information on company production capacity could act as a tool for establishing a matching agency for joint-venture proposals. Sectorally-based research which can identify threats and opportunities is important to meet the new agenda of RDAs. In particular, RDAs may aim to develop local clusters of inter-related industries and firms; protect critical mass of research and development, skills and production capacity in particular sectors to facilitate innovation; and work to develop links between local companies, suppliers and other agencies that tie firms to the area. To support this the research needs to explore supply chains, define benefits of networking, identify critical mass, and identify gaps in capacity where inward investment opportunities should be sought. There is little of this analytical research at a regional level available. Such research, combined with political focus given by the regional chamber, should lead to the identification of a clear set of actions required to achieve the strategy. Local authorities will have a important role in ensuring that key firms in their area input into this research.

Business Support and Changing the Culture – Most discussion in this area has focused on whether there is a need to reform the institutional arrangements. Business Links are currently accountable to GORs, rather than RDAs; many TECs, Business Links and chambers of Commerce have been merging, although a moratorium has currently been put on this process by the government; and the government and LGA are currently reviewing business support services, with the LGA lobbying for more accountability.

However, local authorities also need to discuss what RDAs should be doing in terms of business support. This requires a clear definition of what should be done at the local level, and what at the regional level. The enterprise agency support and generalised personal business adviser services are best delivered at the local level. The approach put forward in this book is that successful European regions are those that develop a learning environment and inter-firm relationships. This requires a cultural change from competition to co-operation and will require public-sector-led business support to develop trust relationships and to facilitate technology transfer and innovation clusters. Developing these new services will be a challenge on which local authorities and RDAs will need to work together.

Technology Strategies and University Links – RDAs are meant to develop technology and innovative strategies and promote technology transfer. The North East has demonstrated through its university network the advantages of getting universities to work co-operatively, provide a 'one-stop shop' and improve access for businesses. RDAs could assist in developing industry and university links. They could also develop a strong regional aspect to the DTI programmes, establishing Regional Foresight Programmes and a regional dimension to the Defence Diversification Agency. Their relationship with GORs and central government, which will remain the implementation arm of regional innovative strategies, will be essential to the success of initiatives in this areas. Government has been very weak in involving local authorities in its work in this area.

In particular benchmarking and mentoring schemes to promote innovation among small- and medium-size industries require local authority support.

Regional Skills Strategies – The Select Committee on Environment, Transport and Regional Affairs argued that RDAs "should control the training budget for their region, plan a regional skills strategy and contract with TECs to carry it out rather than merely assess TECs' contribution towards regional objectives" (Environment, Transport and Regional Affairs Committee, 1998).

The government however has stopped short of giving them these powers, stating: "we will reflect further on the role of RDAs in TEC contracting… when RDAs have had time to establish themselves." (DfEE, 1998).

In the meantime RDAs have been given the task of drawing up regional skills strategies with TECs and national training organisations and the government is providing a skills development fund for this work.

There are some interesting issues here as to whether such strategies will go beyond the current agenda of TECs: whether they will put social exclusion high on the priority list and tackle the demand as well as the supply for labour. This would involve looking at outcomes for disadvantaged groups and at career development paths which would move us beyond the dual labour markets. Local authorities will have a role in pressing for this wider agenda.

Inward Investment and Regional Selective Assistance – There has been a debate over Regional Selective Assistance. The Select Committee on Environment, Transport and Regional Affairs has argued that RDAs should determine applications for RSA rather than simply provide advice to Ministers, while Professor Stephen Fothergill has defended the case for a national strategy that can redistribute funds to Britain's lagging regions. Those local authorities which benefit from RSA will clearly have views on this issue.

In the meantime there remains an issue around the role of inward investment in RDA policy and the appropriate institutional arrangements. In many areas Regional Development Organisations (RDOs) exist which receive considerable financial support from local authorities and are separate companies limited by guarantee with their own boards of directors.

There is a strong case to be made for absorbing RDOs fully into RDAs. This would ensure budgets could be more easily transferred between activities and it would also ensure that aftercare services were integrated with cluster and supply-chain development, avoiding duplication and providing a unified service. Such a merger would also ensure a local authority stake and hence a say in a wider range of RDA activities. In the long term one of the most important functions for RDAs is to take on the control of the Regional Supply Offices. Once this has been achieved the illogicality of having an aftercare service for new companies in a RDO and supply chain and networking support services for existing companies in a RDA will become apparent. However, there are vested interests in RDOs and it will not always be easy to achieve the merger.

Until this happens, local authority board members on Regional Development Organisations will need to ensure that aftercare services are developed which are compatible with the Regional Development Agency strategy.

Land Development – The Urban Regeneration Agency (URA), the statutory form of English Partnerships, will be retained at national level and merged with the Commission for New Towns by 1 April 2000. RDAs will take over the regional staff of English Partnerships and, in the long run, *all* the powers of the URA. There are important issues here for all local authorities and particularly new towns. English Partnerships has acted as a strategic partner and investor in regeneration, with a high priority placed on meeting social objectives through its programmes. On the other hand the predominant task of the Commission for New Towns has been to sell off land to maximise government income, although there have been some exceptions (such as the Invest in Success scheme). In the future local authorities will want to see RDAs acting as regeneration partners in their schemes and prioritising sustainable initiatives which meet social need.

Venture Capital – One of the disappointments in the RDA bill was the limited scope to generate regional financial instruments. The collective borrowing limit on *all* RDAs is £200m (clause 11.6). Yet successful economic regions elsewhere in Europe have developed regional financial instruments which can take a long term view and which can be developed on the basis on reinforcing regional networks and trust. It was for this reason that the Regional Policy Commission recommended "that an incoming Labour government should allow regions to undertake a limited issue of fixed income regional bonds as an experimental regional investment facility" (Regional Policy Commission, 1996) and that these be administered by RDAs (chapter 18). Local authorities may wish to continue to lobby for this but, in the meantime, RDAs can play a useful role in facilitating access to the European Investment Fund (see Holland 1998) and other venture capital sources, encouraging the start-up of new regional venture capital funds through, for example, the partners' pension and superannuation funds.

Utilities Policy – Privatised utilities are key suppliers to local industry so their success and the availability of their products is very much tied in with regional prosperity.

In addition there is considerable evidence from the USA that effective partnerships at regional level can have significant job creation and environmental impact. Policies that reduce demand can often tackle poverty and create jobs (in energy audits, insulation, energy saving products) and limit new capital expenditure (on new power stations, water reservoirs, and so on). But tackling these issues of reducing demand and ensuring good-quality supply for companies, needs a co-ordinated approach at regional level. RDAs have an important, but often neglected, economic role here working with local authorities and utility companies. Local authorities need to consider how they can use planning powers to exert influence (Marvin, Graham and Guy, 1996).

Regeneration – GOR civil servants who dealt with SRB are being transferred to RDAs and the SRB budget is being reformed to develop a more negotiated programme of action in the most deprived areas. It is very unclear how a private sector quango will adapt to this role and how it will empower local communities. Local authorities, as the most important local partnership organisation in regeneration, will need to monitor and record the negotiation process and assess what impact it has on funding programmes and outcomes.

RDAs could play a crucial role in building up community enterprise and making its asset base more secure. Although it is clear that this is a key to the success of community-based enterprise, it will require positive action in capacity building, support and commitment to empowerment.

Liaising with other organisations
What is clear from the discussion above is that, however important the role of RDAs in economic development, they will be ineffective unless they are partnership organisations.

Since they are new organisations, much attention has and will be focused on them. But local authorities will still need to develop relationships with GORs, TECs, Business Links, local FE colleges, and so on, in considering their economic strategies. In addition to their wider roles in economic development, local authorities will need to ensure that the economic development strategy is integrated with planning, environmental and transport strategies. Finally, the respective roles of RDAs and GORs in relation to European funding is far from clear and local authorities will still need to liaise with European, as well as regional, institutions.

Monitoring the Economic Strategies of RDAs
Once the role of RDAs in economic development has been clarified, the monitoring indicators become easier to develop. This

is now the most important task for local authorities, for – unless they establish their scrutiny role through the regional chambers – their influence over the economic agenda will be diminished.

It will be necessary to consider how this evaluation relates to the evaluation of local programmes, such as Single Regeneration Budget, and to the new programmes under the EU structural funds.

The government has established a set of regional competitiveness indicators which are now regularly monitored. These are:

- Gross Domestic Product Per Head (Workplace-based)
- Total Household Disposal Income Per Head
- Manufacturing Labour Productivity (Gross Value Added)
- Business Enterprise R&D for Manufactured Products as a percentage of Gross Value Added
- Percentage of Persons of Working Age in Employment
- Percentage of 19-year-olds with NVQ Level 2 equivalent
- Percentage of workforce qualified to NVQ Level 3
- Percentage of workforce qualified to NVQ Level 4 or above
- Proportion of organisations (with 50+ employees) with Investors in People recognition
- Company start-ups (measured in terms of VAT registration)
- Percentage of businesses surviving 3 years
- Percentage of unemployed persons
- Income Support claimants as percentage of population over 16

There has been a suggestion in some areas that GDP per head is the key indicator and it is important for local authorities to realise the weakness of this indicator and the benefit from looking at a package of indicators. GDP per head tells you nothing about distribution, quality of life, the costs of living in an area – and this affects the real comparative value of GDP, the infrastructure and welfare support available in a region; and the sustainability of the GDP rate. It is a workplace database and gives limited information about residents. Thus, for example, London has a GDP per head rate 40 per cent above the national average. However total household disposable income is less that 20 per cent above the national income, and it has the third highest percentage of income support claimants in the UK and the fourth highest percentage of unemployed. The package of DTI indicators is a considerable improvement on a simplistic GDP per head figure. It also gives some guidance to the key factors that are thought to impact on the competitiveness agenda (that is to say, skill formation, entrepreneurship and R&D investment).

However in terms of monitoring the effectiveness of RDAs there are some important gaps. It may be useful to work towards additional indicators in these areas which would be used in all regions, to aid comparisons. Local authorities may also wish to consider adopting weighted indices to measure the effectiveness of the policies in terms of sustainablility, social inclusion, equality and competitiveness, as has been suggested in The London Study (The Local Futures Group, 1998).

Competitiveness
A key function of the RDA is to develop inter-firm relationships and innovation clusters. This is not measured by the indicators above, which reflect the previous government's competitive agenda as opposed to this government's regional collaborative agenda. Indicators need to be added which reflect the new agenda highlighting the number of networks, joint marketing events, technology transfer, education/university research links, and so on.

Sustainability
There is no measure of environmental sustainability in the competitiveness indicators. If the commitment to sustainability is to become more than a verbal commitment, these indicators need to be high on the agenda. There is a large literature on the type of indicators that can be used.

Social exclusion and inequality
General – The Index of Deprivation gives an overall measure of social exclusion. See also the article by Catherine Howitt and Peter Kenway: 'A Multidimensional Approach to Social Exclusion Indicators' (Oppenheim, 1998).

Poverty in Work – While unemployment and activity rates provide some indication of social exclusion, they fail to deal with poverty in work. There is considerable evidence that temporary, casualised and part-time staff (mostly women) receive limited training by their employers and are often trapped in low-pay jobs. If the RDA training strategies are to go beyond the output data that has dominated TECs, more sophisticated monitoring is required on the impact of the New Deal, the development of career paths and the impact of Investors in People on lower grade staff training opportunities. Individual learning accounts will deliver more information on the supply side of the labour market but for real progress to be made, changes will be required on the demand side of the labour market.

Equal Opportunities – the statistics do not currently reveal different outcomes for gender, race and disability. The monitoring of this has always been shown as a crucial first step to putting in appropriate action to counter social exclusion. There is considerable knowledge of some of the barriers that disadvantage particular groups in the labour market and issues like accessibility, childcare and positive action programmes could also be monitored.

Empowerment – Economic development in deprived neighbourhoods requires holistic and responsive services and the development of community enterprise. Measures to assess the success of these actions need to be placed at the centre of the monitoring of RDAs' work if SRB funds are not to be diverted to business interests.

RECOMMENDATIONS

This section has focused on analysing the complex economic development function of RDAs which has been made more difficult by the fact that DETR powers – rather than DTI and DfEE powers – are being devolved to the agencies.

This section recommends:

- That local authorities and chambers develop a framework for RDA economic strategies linking the key aims of competitiveness, sustainability, equality and inclusion
- That local authorities develop a clear understanding of the nature of the economic development function they expect from RDAs
- In defining the RDA role, local authorities also identify their own role and the nature of partnerships needed to implement the RDA strategies. They will need to use their role, the chamber, Regional Planning Guidance and local authority representation on RDA boards to advance their agenda
- That local authorities work together to develop a set of indicators by which they will, through the chambers, measure and scrutinise RDA performance.

The Implications of RDAs and Regional Strategies for Urban Policy and Sub-regional Partnerships

Stuart Wilks-Heeg,
Research Fellow, European Institute for Urban Affairs,
Liverpool John Moores University

THREE

This contribution considers the likely consequences of the emergence of RDAs for urban policy and sub-regional partnerships. In the past, regional policy has been the prerogative of the Department of Trade and Industry (DTI), and has focussed on inward investment and competitiveness. Urban policy has been with the Department of the Environment, Transport and the Regions (DETR) and has sought to tackle issues of regeneration and deprivation. Up to now these policies have operated separately. Looking at how these two approaches can come together is difficult because, as indicated elsewhere in this publication, the new RDA agenda is evolving rapidly.

Urban policy itself is currently developing a new face within the context of emerging regional policy frameworks, and a White Paper will be published in 1999. Added to this is the fact that the government's commitment to create RDAs has itself provided a fresh impetus for the formation, strengthening and extension of sub-regional partnerships, as key players jockey for position in anticipation of the new agencies.

Despite this fluidity, some reasoned conclusions can be drawn from several recent key policy documents. These include primarily the government's White Paper on Regional Development Agencies, the DETR's discussion paper, *Regeneration Programmes - The Way Forward* (DETR, 1997b), the recent statement made by John Prescott on housing and regeneration policy, the SRB Fifth Round

Bidding Guidance, and the Local Government Association's briefing and guidance notes on the New Commitment to Regeneration (LGA, 1998). Even a cursory glance at these documents makes it clear that despite the numerous shifting policy agendas and the vast range of players, almost all those involved are dancing to the same tune. Common to all of them are the same guiding principles of public-private partnership, of ensuring a balance between physical and social regeneration, and of cross-departmental and cross-sectoral policy-making. This unprecedented level of consensus on basic principles suggests that the future policy agenda may be safely gleaned from these sources.

Within the context of this consensus this section considers the emerging policy agenda in relation to four key issues:

- the likely developments in the overall relationship between specifically urban-based policies and regional strategies
- the changing geographical focus of regeneration policies, particularly the rationale for an explicit 'urban' policy
- the implications of the RDAs for existing partnership arrangements
- the position of the RDAs in relation to resource allocation in regeneration policy.

Urban Policy and the Regional Context

The need for urban policy to operate in a broader regional context is a recurring theme. It has long been recognised that urban economies cannot be divorced from their broader hinterlands and that the spatial reach of any major city's economic and social affairs has steadily grown over the past 30 years. Consequently, it is increasingly evident that the concentration of certain economic and social problems in particular city-districts cannot be understood in isolation from the operation of the surrounding urban system or the wider context of the region. Partly as a result of this realisation and partly as a product of European intervention, public policy in Britain has begun to focus more clearly on cross-sectoral integration at a regional level. In order to be effective, it is therefore important that small-area regeneration goes with the grain of regional economic development, and that it operates within the emergent frameworks of regional governance.

However, despite the creation of the GORs with their role in administering the SRB, a clear regional context for urban policy has remained elusive, as is recognised in a number of recent policy documents. For example, the White Paper on RDAs suggests that economic and social programmes in post-war Britain "have often lacked coherence, particularly at the regional level". Similarly, and with specific reference to urban policy, the DETR's recent discussion paper, *Regeneration Programmes – The Way Forward,* also notes this failure to place urban regeneration in a regional context, suggesting that "only with the supplementary guidance for Round 4 of the Challenge Fund was there a move towards regeneration strategies at the regional level" (DETR, 1997b).

Consequently, recent policy documents have sought to link urban and regional regeneration more explicitly. The bidding guidance for Rounds 4 and 5 of the SRB have laid more stress than previously on the need for bids to relate to the regional context and to the future work of RDAs. Moreover, John Prescott has stated that SRB bids will need to "demonstrate that their local strategies fit within and complement the regional strategies that the RDAs will develop". Similarly, the LGA's *New Commitment to Regeneration* also lays stress on the need to make connections with the role of RDAs. The Local Government Association's New Commitment to Regeneration is a pilot scheme initiated by local government which seeks to explore ways of achieving regeneration through improved integration of mainstream services. It has been enthusiastically received by local authorities and central government alike and is likely to provide an important input into current and future urban policy debates.

Given that this drive to integrate urban and regional policies comes from a number of quarters, it may be assumed that this will in future be a key priority for policy-makers at the national, regional and local levels.

The RDAs and the Geographical Focus of Regeneration Policy

In recent years there has also been a blurring of the definition and boundaries of urban policy as regeneration initiatives have cast their net wider than the earlier concern with the so-called 'inner-cities'. This trend was particularly evident with the launch of the SRB which has enabled the GORs to fund regeneration schemes in any part of the country. Despite the recent decision to target the SRB more directly at deprived areas, the RDAs are likely to accelerate this shift towards regarding 'regeneration' as a general policy concern, rather than one specific to certain urban areas. These new agencies will be expected to direct regeneration policy at strategic sites across their respective regions, linking these separate initiatives into a broader regional framework. The biggest potential barrier to such a development will be the possibility of central government interference. The White Paper suggests that the capacity to determine the balance between regionally- and locally-based initiatives will remain in the hands of central government ("Ministers will define the balance between action on region-wide programmes or regional strategic sites and support of local partnerships and programmes"). However, it is likely that, since the RDAs will be operating 'on the ground', they will, in reality, have significant opportunity to direct this process.

Given that regeneration policies are no longer specific to the inner-cities, a subsequent issue is the spatial scale at which regeneration policy will be directed under the RDAs. Until now urban policy initiatives have almost always been based on small-area regeneration. However, Jeremy Beecham, chair of the LGA, has argued that the SRB as a locally-based policy initiative fits uncomfortably with the remit of the RDAs. As a result, Beecham has proposed renaming the SRB the 'Single Regional Budget' and giving it a remit to focus on larger geographical areas. While many in local government would welcome such an approach, a regional bias to regeneration policy may favour more purely economic, rather than community-based, regeneration, particularly where RDAs are dominated by private-sector interests.

The RDAs and Sub-regional Partnerships

The launch of both City Challenge and its successor, the SRB, reflect a growing consensus about the importance of partnership in regeneration policy. Driven initially by a desire to secure additional funding, partnership formation has increasingly taken on its own dynamic, particularly around economic regeneration initiatives at a sub-regional level. However, while sub-regional partnerships have, to date, promoted themselves well, their role should not be overestimated. And many remain more local than regional in their orientation.

Nonetheless there is no reason to suppose that the creation of RDAs, and the transfer of responsibility for the SRB to them, will upset this core consensus. Indeed, since the RDA boards will, in themselves, be composed of individuals from across the private, public and voluntary sectors, the trend will clearly be one of strengthening the partnership approach. Moreover, since partnerships have become increasingly typical of local governance and RDAs will only possess the capacity to advise and exert influence in several key policy areas, it is likely that inter-agency networks will also become the key feature of governance at the regional level. Such partnerships do already exist in some areas, although primarily at a sub-regional rather than regional level. And many weaker partnerships have been prompted by the formation of RDAs into taking steps to strengthen their capacities.

The creation of RDAs is therefore likely to lead to a more comprehensive emergence of multi-level partnerships, operating at the regional, sub-regional and local levels respectively. However, there is no reason to suppose that these partnerships will fit neatly inside one another like Russian dolls. Instead, many of the partnerships will overlap. Some may have conflicting outlooks and agendas. And there will be instances where issues of accountability and transparency will become a major concern, certainly until regional chambers, or perhaps even regional parliaments, become a reality. In the meantime the RDAs will need to make sense of these overlapping partnerships. However, given the very real concerns about accountability, the task of shaping them into coherent regional regeneration strategies should fall to the chambers.

The RDAs and Regeneration Resources

The RDAs will preside over increased financial resources dedicated to regeneration initiatives. Following the Comprehensive Spending Review a total of £2.3bn will be made available through the SRB, the key regeneration budget controlled by the RDAs, over the next three years. However, given that the RDAs will not, at least initially, have the capacity to *vire* funds, the scope for the new bodies to supplement these resources with contributions from other budgets will be limited. Regrettably, the opportunity to use the RDAs to achieve closer integration between the SRB and Regional Selective Assistance has been lost, as has the hope that the RDAs would be able to influence the activities of the TECs, as both will remain in the remit of the Whitehall departments.

Changes to the way in which SRB resources are allocated have also been announced. Eighty per cent of resources will be targeted on the most deprived local authorities, while allowing other authorities to bid for the remaining twenty per cent. However, allocation through competitive bidding, now an acknowledged feature of urban governance, will continue to play a role. The RDAs will therefore be required to allocate regeneration resources on the basis of both deprivation indicators and inter-authority competition.

Beyond this the RDAs should find that they are largely permitted to decide how SRB resources are allocated. Although the White Paper states that the RDAs will only be able to make recommendations to ministers about the funding of regeneration projects, it seems unlikely that ministers will fundamentally alter these decisions. It is perhaps because of the obvious issues of accountability surrounding the RDAs that the government has retained a degree of reserve power over where and how SRB funds are spent. However, government ministers have not to date made any significant objections to the GOR's allocation of SRB funds. While they may initially monitor the RDAs' decisions closely, the RDAs should find that if they attempt to direct funding in a manner which encourages a more strategic, regional approach to regeneration, they will be pushing at an open door.

Conclusion

Despite the fluidity of the current situation, every sign suggests that the end product will constitute the most serious attempt yet to place and co-ordinate regeneration initiatives within a coherent regional framework. Despite their shortcomings and a degree of uncertainty about their exact role, the RDAs represent an unprecedented opportunity to achieve a more strategic approach to regeneration at the regional level. They will therefore be at the forefront of the drive towards a more integrated and comprehensive approach to regeneration based on multi-level partnerships.

The RDAs are perhaps not the radical policy departure many had hoped for; in many ways they represent a logical extension to the policies of the previous government, rather than a change from them. Yet the experience of the GORs, introduced by the Major government in 1994, would appear to suggest that the RDAs can make a difference. Whether they do so will depend critically on the quality of their leadership and the capacity of those leaders to ally with existing proponents of strategic regional intervention and minimise needless duplication and overlap. Once they have made this critical first step, the potential for them to gain more significant policy responsibilities and executive powers, alongside a gradual democratisation of the emergent structures of regional governance, will increase substantially.

RECOMMENDATIONS

This contribution has stressed that the precise policy frameworks linking the RDAs, sub-regional partnerships and urban policy will emerge over the next few years. However, in the meantime there are a number of ways in which local authorities can seek to play a constructive role in this process, including:

- using their voice in regional chambers to ensure that the development of regional regeneration frameworks does not come at the expense of suitable systems of democratic accountability
- continuing to mobilise more coherent sub-regional and

regional partnerships so that local authorities are in a stronger position to express collectively their views on regional policy and on the allocation of SRB resources

- monitoring the RDAs to ensure that regeneration does not become too narrowly focused on economic development
- promoting examples, drawn particularly from the LGA's *New Commitment* initiative, of how successful integration of public policies can contribute to more effective regeneration initiatives
- making local authority experience of public-private partnership formation available to the RDAs, with a particular focus on disseminating models of best practice
- working together with RDAs to build up powerful regional alliances which will constitute a wedge against any future governmental centralisation.

Regional Development Agencies and Europe

Adrian Colwell,
European and International Affairs Officer,
Convention of Scottish Local Authorities

T his section examines the issues relating to the establishment of the new Regional Development Agencies and their relationship to policy matters deriving from the European Union. It is divided into two main sections: the relationship to the structural funds, and the relationship to other related EU issues. Finally, there are a number of recommendations for action by local authorities over the coming months.

FOUR

Relationship to the structural funds

The government is proposing that the new RDAs which are to take up their powers on 1 April 1999, should play a significant role in relation to the new European structural fund programmes established for the period 2000 to 2006.

The White Paper *Building Partnership for Prosperity* (December 1997) notes: "Regional Development Agencies will have a strong European dimension..." (Para 9.5) "The structural funds, and other forms of European funding, will continue to play an important role in regional competitiveness and social policy in the English regions... the government intends that RDAs should take a leading role in the new programmes in the English regions..." (Para 7.6) (DETR, 1997a).

The UK government's agenda is matched by that of the European Commission which set out its policy priority for the next period of European regional policy in a document called *Agenda 2000* (Commission of the European Communities, 1997). This document sets out the European Commission's proposals for the financing of the European Union in the 2000-2006 period. It contains major proposals for the re-ordering of EU policies – such as the structural funds and the Common Agricultural Policy (CAP) – and details the process for starting the negotiations which will lead to the enlargement of the EU from the year 2002 onwards. In particular, both the European Commission and the UK government have stressed their priorities as being to promote regional competitiveness.

Agenda 2000 states: "The structural funds should aim at fostering competitive development and sustainable and job-creating growth throughout the Union and the promotion of a skilled, trained and adaptable workforce."

For the UK government, the Minister of State Richard Caborn has noted: "RDAs will be an essential first step to enable the regions to improve their competitiveness and to provide for effective, properly co-ordinated regional economic development." (11 June 1997).

It is also clear that both the European Commission and the UK government are proposing the development of comprehensive regional strategies. It is in the overall interest of policy coherence that these two sets of strategies are established in a way that reinforces and supports the activities and objectives proposed in each.

The European Commission's *Agenda 2000* document makes reference to the process of developing new structural fund programmes as including the preparation of an "integrated strategy for economic diversification" (Vol.1, p.20).

The UK government has proposed that the new Regional Development Agencies will address a number of themes which are consistent with EU policy objectives and include:

- economic development and regeneration
- competitiveness, business support and investment
- skills support
- employment creation
- sustainable development.

These themes will contribute to the establishment of a single regional strategy which is an essential first step to accessing – and then to the successful use of – EU structural funds. Under the Conservative government there was no effective regional policy to address the differing needs of the English regions and in this situation, access to the EU structural funds led by English local authorities effectively acted as a substitute. The new Labour government has proposed the creation of RDAs as organisations able to marshal resources and policies that are capable of addressing these different regional needs.

As the DETR have already noted, "...regeneration activity works best where there is a single strategy or hierarchy of strategies". (*Regeneration Programmes – the Way Forward,* DETR 1997b).

While the RDAs start their work on 1 April 1999, their ability to influence the current structural fund programmes will be limited.

The current programmes will run until December 1999 or June 2000 and have detailed strategies and application procedures already in place, which the RDAs will not be able to change. These programmes will, however, constitute a source of additional funding to support eligible RDA activities in the first year of operation. They also represent a significant policy mechanism, which is already in place for much of England, on which the new RDAs should build.

The real advantage of establishing the RDAs will arise in the period of the structural funds 2000-2006. While the negotiations on the new structural fund regulations are not expected to be completed until April or May 1999, and are subject to complex negotiations between the Council of Ministers (all 15 Member-state governments), and the European Commission and the European parliament, parts of the likely outcome are already clear:

- Many parts of England currently eligible for structural fund support will continue to do so for a new seven-year programme period. Many of the industrial, urban, rural and fishery areas will continue to be fully eligible and any area losing full status will continue to have access to programmes on a transitional basis of at least four years and possibly six years, depending on the outcome of the negotiations in Brussels
- New programmes will need to be developed for approval after

the structural fund regulations have been agreed and to ensure that there is not a programme delay to the start of new programmes from 1 January 2000 onwards

- The new structural fund programmes will continue to be governed by programme partnerships which will involve local authorities, colleges, TECs, NGOs and other bodies. The RDAs should aim to enter these partnerships as *equals,* not leaders.

  It is these programme partnerships which approve eligible projects for funding

- European structural funding will continue to be additional (or extra) on top of the resources committed to projects by the RDA's and other programme partners.

- There will be a commitment in the new structural fund programme period to access new sources of finance, such as loan guarantee, venture capital support to ensure that the limited public resources and limited European funding goes as far as possible. Public-private partnerships will also be promoted, and strict monitoring and evaluation procedures will help to ensure that public money is well spent.

The European Commission has already begun to consider how the relationship between the RDAs and new structural fund programmes should be established. It is clear that as a major regional body a close working relationship and participation in the programming partnerships, which are established to run European regional programmes, will be expected.

When the RDAs start in April 1999, they will need to very quickly establish close working relationships with existing programme partners, local authorities and others to prepare the European programmes which are to run in eligible areas over the 2000-2006 period. Many areas will continue to be fully eligible for a seven-year period and those losing status will have access to transitional support for a minimum period of four years. The work on the new European strategies *must start now.* (It should be noted that programmes will be invited to be submitted to the Commission from eligible areas and areas in transition, six months after the completion of the negotiations on the regulations which are not expected to be concluded until April or May 1999.) This will help to ensure all partner priorities are reflected in the new programmes, to avoid a delay in starting the programmes and to ensure that the RDAs do not have to start with a 'blank sheet of paper' and with only a few months in which to co-ordinate the development and negotiation of the new programmes. This approach has already been implicitly acknowledged by the UK government. On 11 November 1997 the Minister of State Richard Caborn noted: "I want to see a more collaborative approach and shared understanding of strategies and priorities" (launch of *The Way Forward for Regeneration*).

The European Commission have already given an indication of the format of the new structural fund regional strategies. The points below illustrate the content that the Commission would like to see addressed.

THE STUCTURE OF NEW STRUCTURAL FUND PROGRAMMES 2000 - 2006

- Quantified description of current economic situation in the region

- Description of the strategy to be pursued, including details of:
    - quantified objectives
    - development priorities
    - the geographic areas as whole.

- Prior appraisal of what the proposed strategy will achieve, including:
    - economic impacts
    - environmental impacts
    - social impacts, including employment effects.

- Results of consultations with:
    - competent authorities and bodies (such as local authorities, NGOs, and environmental bodies)
    - economic and social partners.

- Indicative overall financial table (this would follow the

completion of the negotiations on the draft regulations in 1999)

- Description of measures to provide the framework for project development and selection criteria

- Information on the need for:
    - studies (to ensure the strategy continues to address identified regional needs and economic trends)
    - demonstration projects (which might promote innovative new approaches)
    - training for partners to ensure high quality projects and responding to new policy developments
    - technical assistance to support operations.

- Designation of competent authorities and responsible bodies. (Detailing the role of partner organisations, their decision making powers and the responsibilities of partners to avoid fraud, and to develop monitoring and evaluation and efficient programme systems)

- Provisions to ensure effective and correct implementation through:
    - monitoring and evaluation
    - definition of quantified indicators for evaluation
    - arrangements for controls and sanctions
    - adequate programme publicity

Source: Presentation to COSLA Conference, June 1998, by Robin Liddel: European Commission

It is clear that many of these issues will also be addressed in the formulation of the new RDA strategies. It is expected that the RDAs and the new structural fund programmes will cover the same geographical areas: West Midlands, North East England, and so on.

The key questions for the development of the new structural fund strategies and RDA strategies are the same and a close relationship is essential, though two documents will be necessary. The questions to be asked address:

- How to make the regional economy more competitive
- How to regenerate the physical and social fabric of the region

- How to improve the skills base of the region
- How to promote and create new jobs
- How to ensure a balanced regeneration of urban and rural areas
- How to respect the principles of equal opportunities and sustainable development.

Considering the development of the two strategies at the same time will ensure that the EU and UK resources can complement each other and achieve a joint impact and result in strengthened partnerships.

As a recent commentator has noted: "regions have realised the need for an overarching strategy for economic development in each region and have also developed ideas about the importance of long term partnerships which are not just put together to seek funds". (Dungey, 1997).

The RDAs and local/regional partners will need to ensure their experience is pooled and that existing strategies are built on and the relationship fully described in the European programme text. The most relevant existing regional strategies include:

- Local Agenda 21 Strategies
- Regional Technology Plans
- The National Employment Action Plans
- Tourism Strategies
- Business Links
- Regional Planning Guidance.

The success or failure of the new RDAs will be, in part, a result of the attitude adopted by partner organisations such as local authorities. Starting the process of planning for the new European programmes before the establishment of the RDAs will give the RDAs a head start; and help to ensure that implementation of the new structural fund programmes are driven by regional partnership priorities and not those of the European Commission.

It is essential that this work commences as soon as possible.

Other Related EU Issues

It is clear that over time there will be a need for the role of the RDAs and chambers to evolve to match developments at the EU level. The need for an evolutionary approach has already been noted in earlier considerations of the need to establish powerful agencies in the English regions.

"Without regional representatives to match, for example, the German Länder and the powerful Spanish regions, there is a risk that the better-developed regionalism on the Continent will eclipse English regions' ability to influence future policy" (Murphy and Caborn, 1995).

The RDAs and chambers will need to consider how to address the impact of other EU issues on the development of the regional economy. These include:

- the impact of strengthened EU commitment to sustainability, which has followed the adoption of the Amsterdam Treaty and will influence the preparation of the Sixth Environmental Action Programme due to be drafted 1999-2000. This will set out the framework for EU environmental policy concerning noise, water and air pollution, extending the scope of the Environmental Impact Assessment and the relationship to regional, urban and rural policy.
- the impact of the forthcoming reform of the Common Agricultural Policy and the moves to establish a comprehensive rural development framework. As the reform process initiated by the EU *Agenda 2000* document has noted, "the development of rural areas should build better links between countryside and local towns". (Vol.1, p.21).
- the impact of the changes to Assisted Area coverage in England which result from the implementation of the European Commission Communication on National Aid (OJC 74 10 March 1998). Once agreed in March 1999 the Communication will reduce the population eligible for coverage under Assisted Area status, and have an impact on regions access to Regional Selective Assistance to support the attraction of foreign direct investment and the amounts of aid

which can be provided. The RDAs will need to ensure that their regeneration is consistent with EU State Aid rules, covering support for research and development, training and business development.

- the RDAs will need to ensure that they are aware of the changing EU policy regime for small and medium-sized enterprises, public procurement, and finance available from the EU research and development programmes.
- as EU enlargement takes in more of eastern Europe, opportunities will increase for participation by public organisations such as RDAs to collaborate on the East-West development programmes; as well as ensuring that small and medium-sized enterprises, and other businesses, are prepared to take advantage of the opportunities presented in an enlarged European Single Market.
- the RDAs will also need to ensure that their policies and programmes for skills support and training reflect and complement the implementation of the National Employment Action Programme (NEAP). The Treaty of Amsterdam included a new Employment chapter which led to the establishment of annual NEAPs being agreed to between each member state and the European Commission. It is anticipated that, from 2000 onwards, funds available under the European Social Fund to support training initiatives will have a strong regional focus and will require a close collaboration between the RDAs, local authorities, TECs and colleges on the development and implementation of the most appropriate regional training strategies.
- the relationship of Members of the European Parliament(MEPs) to the new regional structures and programmes needs to be considered. With the introduction of a new system of proportional representation, MEPs are now elected on the same regional boundaries as the GORs. This gives greater potential for MEPs to pursue a clearly regional agenda. Local authorities will also wish to consider how best to liaise with them. Consideration also needs to be given to representation on the EU Committee of the Regions, and

whether representatives should report and be accountable to the local government regional body or the chamber.

RECOMMENDATIONS

Local authorities must start their preparation of the new European regional strategies, together with other regional partners. The issues which should be considered include:

- identifying baseline economic indicators
- establishing the economic and social development priorities for the 2000 - 2006 European programmes and assessing the anticipated economic, social and environmental impact of the proposed strategies
- detailing the links to other existing regional strategies
- ensuring full consultation with existing programme partners
- examining how new EU policy priorities such as employment creation, sustainability and social exclusion should be addressed within the new structural fund programmes.

Local authorities should consider how the wider European issues set out in this section could be addressed in the regional partnerships in which the RDAs will be involved.

Regional Chambers: the Example of Yorkshire and Humberside

Liz Kerry,
Director, Regional Assembly for Yorkshire and Humberside

In July 1996 the 22 local authorities in Yorkshire and Humberside came together, in cross-party agreement, to form the Regional Assembly for Yorkshire and Humberside – the region's local authority grouping.

The Regional Assembly brought together the work of three pre-existing structures: the Regional Planning Conference, the Yorkshire and Humberside Regional Association and the European Office. Its purpose is to promote democratic, locally elected leadership by:

- promoting the economic, social and environmental well-being of the region for the benefit of all its people
- working strategically and in partnership
- bringing coherence
- observing subsidiarity.

It acts as a strategic body and concerns itself with those issues that benefit from taking a regional perspective and which cannot effectively be dealt with at a local authority level.

During it first year of operation, the Regional Assembly's main priorities were to establish its credibility as the voice of local government, within the region, at a national level and in Europe; to be recognised as a key force in promoting the interests of Yorkshire and Humberside, and to position itself as a leading partner in developing and driving an agenda which would secure the future prosperity of the region.

At the time, Yorkshire and Humberside was fragmented both

geographically and organisationally, with the second lowest GDP per head of any of the English regions.

Although there was a lot of activity taking place in areas such as business support, health, education and regeneration, the key policy decisions that were being taken across a range of agencies were largely un-coordinated. In addition, huge resources were being handled in the region by agencies (TECs, the police, the health service) accountable, not to the local communities that they served, but nationally or to Ministers.

This gap, identified as constituting a democratic deficit, raised questions about where and how decisions were being taken and what influence local people could have on these. It pointed up concern about the regional coherence of decisions being taken between different agencies, the investment of their resources and their priorities.

Advancing Together - a strategic framework

Recognising the importance of having key players in the region pull together in the same direction, the Regional Assembly began to develop strong working relationships with partners and stakeholders from the private, public and voluntary sectors and to lead, through the Yorkshire and Humberside Partnership, a wide-ranging, inclusive consultation process.

Over a 15-month period, between February 1997 and April 1998 the partners examined existing strategies to see how the work of each contributed to the overall picture and to identify needs and gaps in provision in the region.

This process led to agreeing a shared vision for the region and securing the commitment of partners working to achieve it.

It culminated in the production of *Advancing Together* a strategic framework for the region which promotes a vision of Yorkshire and Humberside as "a world-class region, where the economic, environmental and social well-being of all our people is advancing more rapidly and more sustainably than our competitors."

Advancing Together outlines five clear strategic objectives:

- an advanced economy
- a robust infrastructure
- sustainable environments
- a skilled and flexible workforce
- an enhanced quality of life for all

It recognises the importance of the links between actions and policies and between economic, environmental and social factors. It has broad based support from all sectors, and embraces a wide range of policy areas – health, housing, crime, culture and bio-diversity as well as the economy. It also acknowledges the degree of co-ordination required to successfully bring about coherence in policy and manage the region.

One of the core values integrating this wide-ranging agenda is sustainability – promoting sustainable development through achieving a balance between economic, environmental and social needs, a key factor of which is spatial planning and the new style Regional Planning Guidance which is being lead by the local authority sector.

Alongside this important and growing local agenda, within Europe, the Regional Assembly started to enter and influence some of the big policy debates about issues that would affect the region, such as the reform of the Common Agricultural Policy and European structural funds.

The National Agenda and the RDAs

At a national level, a new government had been elected and was undertaking a large number of wide ranging policy reviews and consultations. The Regional Assembly made responses to a variety of these, including those on health, crime, the future of Regional Planning Guidance and Fundamental Spending Reviews.

Also, within months of their election, the government published the White Paper *Building Partnerships for Prosperity* (DETR, 1997a). which set out plans for nine Development Agencies aimed at improving economic performance in the English regions.

While welcoming the overall approach of the White Paper, within the local government sector there was disappointment that the government had not taken the opportunity to address the democratic deficit by creating statutory regional chambers to take on a wide range of functions currently undertaken by unelected and locally unaccountable bodies or by remote authorities in Whitehall or Westminster. This disappointment was all the greater given that the new Development Agencies themselves were to be accountable to Ministers rather than at regional level.

Strong lobbying by the Regional Assembly and the local government sector nationally failed to persuade the government to establish chambers which would have the power to hold the RDAs to account.

However, the White Paper did create an opportunity for regional voluntary chambers to apply to Ministers to become the designated body with which the RDA should consult, and this has followed through into the legislation.

The Regional Chamber for Yorkshire and Humberside

The earlier work of the Regional Assembly and its partners, had positioned Yorkshire and Humberside to take advantage of this opportunity. In March 1998, with Royal Assent to the RDA Bill still some months away, the Regional Assembly, its partners and other regional stakeholders made a firm public commitment to work together for the future development of the region, and launched the first regionalchamber in England, the significance of which was marked by the presence of the deputy prime minister, John Prescott.

The local-authority-led regional chamber is a new, high-level, strategic partnership which formally brings together the key stakeholders in the region to promote the economic, social and environmental well-being of everybody who lives and works in the region.

It provides a single voice for Yorkshire and Humberside and reinforces the links between the public, private and voluntary sectors to ensure that the region's future development has broad-based commitment and ownership.

Membership of the chamber includes representatives of all 22 local authorities, the CBI, the Association of Yorkshire and Humberside Chambers of Commerce, the Regional TUC, Yorkshire and Humberside TECs, the Churches' Regional Commission, the health sector, the Yorkshire and Humberside Cultural Forum, the Yorkshire Rural Community Council, the Yorkshire and Humberside Universities Association, the Police Services, the Environment Agency, the Yorkshire and Humberside Association of Colleges, and the Regional Forum for Voluntary and Community Organisations, with input from the Government Office for Yorkshire and the Humber, and, when established, the Regional Development Agency as observers.

The regional chamber is committed to working in a transparent and open manner. It needs and embraces a wide range of organisations in a way that makes room for everybody in shaping the future of Yorkshire and Humberside.

At its inaugural meeting on 20 July, the regional chamber endorsed and adopted *Advancing Together* as its agenda for action. It elected its first Chair, Cllr Brian Walker, Leader of Leeds City Council, and, until recently, Chair of the Regional Assembly. He sees the chamber as the driving force in getting the region to pull together towards the same objectives and in leading the pursuit of the vision and the development of the integrated framework. It will secure the necessary commitment from partners to deliver it, identify priorities for the future, monitor progress towards the agreed objectives and feed back into the framework to take account of changing needs.

The chamber will be seeking designation by Ministers as the key regional body for consultation by the RDA, thus beginning to address the democratic deficit.

And while the RDA's objectives concentrate on economic development and regeneration, employment and the development of skills, the chamber is about trying to get consensus about what the region needs to do in a whole range of areas, including the social and environmental agendas, recognising the links between them and then ensuring delivery.

With the appointment of the chair, board and chief executive of the RDA, the new regional mechanisms are rapidly taking shape.

The development of these regional structures needs to be viewed within the context of the government's wider, and far-reaching agenda for change. Local authorities' response to modernising local government will have an important influence on the way in which they interact with regional structures.

The Regional Assembly will continue as the local government grouping for the region and will play a leading role in the development of the Chamber's policy, particularly in regard to sustainability and maintaining the integration that underpins it.

It will also continue to play an active part in shaping local government policy at national level on a wide range of issues. It will maintain its crucial role in relation to the integrated transport strategy and spatial planning through the regional planning conference and it is keen to use the regional chamber as a forum through which local authorities can consult wider interests in, for example, the preparation of new-style regional planning guidance.

It remains the only democratically elected regional body, albeit indirectly elected, which can legitimately scrutinise the operations of public utilities, government agencies and other unelected public bodies operating at regional level.

As the government's agenda for the English regions begins to take shape, the relationship between the regional assembly, regional chamber and Regional Development Agency becomes crucial. It needs to be complementary and mutually supportive with all three working closely together towards common goals for the future development of the region.

The present government has expressed its commitment to directly elected regional government where there is demand for it. Whether or not this will happen in the immediate future remains to be seen. In the meantime, the region remains an important unit in Europe, in competitiveness terms and as a force for social cohesion. New regional structures still have a lot of work to do in addressing a local and rapidly increasing agenda.

Conclusion

This section has focussed on Yorkshire and Humberside as an example of how regional structures are developing to meet both the government agenda and local needs.

Other English regions are developing similar – although by no means identical – structures at their own pace and to meet their own circumstances. The regional chamber is now the key regional partnership in Yorkshire and Humberside and its relationship with the RDA and other regional bodies will be critical in moving forward a complex and rapidly changing agenda.

Although these regional mechanisms are not as clear as those of the directly elected structures in Scotland and Wales, the indirectly elected assemblies and chambers, working alongside the Regional Development Agencies, can at least start to address the economic and democratic deficits which have existed in the English regions for far too long.

The West Midlands: Taking Forward the Regional Agenda

Andrew Coulson, Senior Lecturer, Institute for Local Government Studies, University of Birmingham; and a member of Birmingham City Council

O f all the English regions, the West Midlands has the most developed and extensive institutional arrangements for regional governance. Yet few policymakers outside the region are aware of its strengths, and of the pressures these are creating for more democratically accountable regional government.

Developing regional structures

The key has been the transformation of the West Midlands Regional Forum of Local Authorities – the body which co-ordinated local authority planning, transport and economic development policies across the region – into an active and effective regional branch of the Local Government Association.

The creation of the Government Office for the West Midlands in 1995, the commitment of the Labour opposition to devolution to Scotland and Wales and regional institutions in England, and the prospect of a unified Local Government Association representing all types of local authority, enabled attention to be given to how the Forum should be extended to give every district and unitary authority proper representation. In the Spring of 1997 the following were agreed:

- Each shire district would have one representative in a new body, the West Midlands Local Government Association (WMLGA)
- Each county would have the same number of representatives as

its districts
- The seven metropolitan districts would have, in total, the same numbers as the non-metropolitan areas; where there was more than a single representative from one council, representation would follow the proportionality rules for local authority committees
- Unitary authorities were treated in the same way as metropolitan districts
- If only a limited number of delegates for one council was present at any meeting, then those present could cast the votes for their whole party group from that council.

The WMLGA is an indirectly elected assembly comprising 120 elected delegates, 60 from the metropolitan district (21 of these from Birmingham), 24 from the shire districts, 24 from the four shire counties, and 12 from the three unitaries. Subscriptions are pro-rata with membership. A structure of committees has been created, broadly reflecting that of the national LGA:

- Co-ordinating Committee (26)
- Regeneration and Environment (120)
- Human Resources (120)
- European and International affairs (120)
- Housing and Environmental Health (68)
- Leisure and Tourism (68)
- Social Affairs and Health (36)
- Education and Training (36)

It was agreed that the chairs of these committees should rotate between different types of council.

For a year the regional LGA ran alongside the West Midlands Forum. The two merged, on 1 April 1998, with the planning and transport responsibilities of the Forum taken on by the Regeneration and Environment Committee of the LGA. The West Midlands Employers' Organisation and the Provincial Council also joined together, re-emerging as the Human Resources Committee of the LGA. At the time of writing there is a lobby for a Public

Protection Committee, bringing together trading standards, police and community safety, fire and emergency planning.

There was debate as to who should clerk the new organisation for its initial period. It was agreed that this would rotate among types of authority. The districts expressed preference for a metropolitan district for the first two years, and the seven chief executives got together and decided that Birmingham should fulfil this role. This meant that the resources of the City Council's corporate strategy unit and legal services were available at a crucial time. A major figure for the region was appointed as a chief executive – Sid Platt, previously head of the West Midlands Regional TUC.

The new organisation took over the negotiating responsibilities of the West Midlands Employers' Organisation (which had built up expertise on single status agreements, CCT, best value, and so on). It was also able to draw on work of the partnerships fostered by the West Midlands Forum over the previous decade, which had produced a regional competitiveness framework and action plan, a framework for Regional Planning Guidance, transportation strategy, and a European strategy. It already had an office in Brussels – created out of the office formerly run by Birmingham, headed by the former European officer for the four Black Country boroughs. Its relationship with the Government Office on all these matters was excellent.

This new structure was developed in the run up to the 1997 general election, influenced by the thinking that lay behind some of the proposals of Jack Straw. The LGA would become the regional assembly – indirectly elected initially, but hopefully directly elected within a few years. The Government Office would become its executive, that is to say, be made politically accountable to the Assembly – with a similar relationship to that of the Welsh Office to the National Assembly for Wales. The Development Agency would be a relatively small arms-length company, incorporating English Partnerships, the West Midlands Development Agency (the regional inward investment agency) and perhaps the West Midlands Enterprise Board (set up with similar intentions in 1982 by the West Midlands County Council, and still in existence, largely working on economic consultancy). Private sector equity partners – such as

investment banking arms of commercial banks or pension funds –
might also be involved. This body would be the investment agency
of the Assembly – holding land, creating company structures to
make best use of investment resources for Europe or elsewhere,
meeting the needs both of potential inward investors and of local
companies that needed new sites, management or equity partners.
The structure is shown in Figure 1.

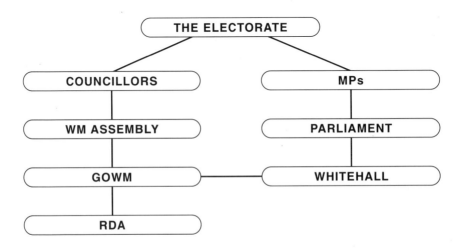

Figure 1: A theoretical structure for regional governance

The government's proposals

But this was not to be, at least for the time being and in that form.
The Queen's Speech drafted within a day or two of the 1997
election victory included commitments to Regional Development
Agencies backed by regional chambers with strong representation
from business, but no legislation to alter the status of the
Government Offices. The consultation document suggested that
the RDAs would be non-departmental public bodies, quangos with
their boards appointed by the Secretary of State for the
Environment, Transport and the Regions; and only a minority from

local government, and a majority from private business. They were to take direct responsibility for the work of English Partnerships and the Single Regeneration Budget.

The Departments of Trade and Industry and of Education and Employment decided initially not to delegate responsibility for Training and Enterprise Councils, Business Links, Regional Selective Assistance, or European regional investment. The new RDAs will be less overtly corporate than the Government Offices where DTI, DfEE and DETR civil servants work together in the same building, co-ordinated by the Regional Director. The regional chamber would have strong business representation, and this body, rather than the regional LGA (or Assembly-in-waiting) would give political direction to the RDA. Figure 2, prepared by Sandy Taylor of Birmingham City Council, shows how the situation might look, post-1999:

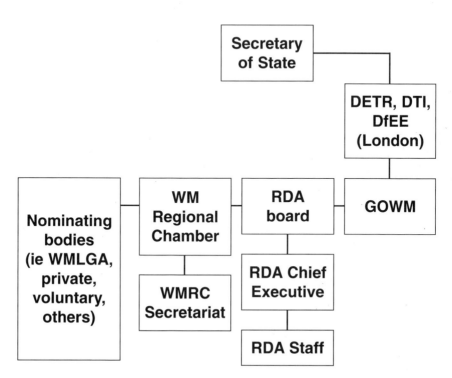

Figure 2: West Midlands RDA Mechanisms, post-April 1999

The announcement that priority in terms of legislation would be given to RDAs, and not to democratic accountability through regional institutions, was not what most people in the region expected. But the partnerships were already in place to respond to any proposal. The West Midlands response to the consultation on RDAs proposed that they should be extremely powerful, taking responsibility for regional budgets for training held by the TECs (and perhaps also the Further Education Funding Council), all European regional programmes, and regional quangos. If this went ahead there would be little left for the Government Office! The government was much more cautious, and will leave the two alongside each other the RDA working with and consulting a regional chamber while formally reporting to the Secretary of State.

The likely option now is for a regional chamber of 60, with 70 per cent of its membership from local authorities. Some of the private sector partners would like a smaller chamber and more private sector involvement. The West Midlands Chamber is expected to be in place before the end of 1998. By this time the WMLGA will be even more established.

Strengths of the West Midlands

It is clear that the West Midlands has the building blocks in place for a rapid progress towards elected regional government, once it can persuade central government to give it the green light. It benefits from having an undisputed centre – Birmingham – in contrast to the rivalry between Manchester and Liverpool, or Leeds and Sheffield, and the debate about whether Bristol is an appropriate capital for the South West, or whether Cumbria is in the Northern or North-Western region. Birmingham City Council has acted diplomatically, offering services but not insisting on leadership or special privileges. People in the area have a consciousness as Midlanders or Brummies. Birmingham and the conurbation is the second city, and so needs to assert itself against the claims of London on the one hand, and Manchester on the other. It is unambiguously the heartland of British manufacturing – and hence has strong employers' organisations and regional companies. It is also next to Wales, which means that the most deprived rural parts of the West Midlands can see what organisations such as the Welsh Development Agency can deliver.

Brian Hogwood has pointed out that the West Midlands Government Office boundary – the seven metropolitan districts and four surrounding counties – is already used for administrative purposes by most government departments and many quangos such as West Midlands Arts, more so than any other Government Office of the Region. It has helped that, for the time being, the great majority of the councils in the region are under moderate Labour control or hung councils where Labour has considerable influence. Last but not least the head of the Government Office, David Ritchie, was an experienced and respected civil servant, familiar with the region, prepared to get involved in detailed work, but also very committed to moving forward the agenda for regional governance.

Looking to the future

It is hard to believe that the structure of institutions that will be in place by early 1999 will survive for long. It may atrophy as parts prove ineffectual. Or fly apart in a blaze of acrimony as the various chief executives, chairs and heads fall out with each other over the best solutions to some of the deep-seated problems facing the region (such as whether to build or expand roads, make large industrial sites available in the green belt, pour money into land reclamation, and where and on what scale to build new houses). Most likely - and optimistically – it will hold together long enough for something more coherent to be put in place – a structure that is clear to the voters of the West Midlands, convincing to the business community, and can claim a track record of both job creation, raising levels of education and skills, finding effective responses to social exclusion, and protection/enhancement of the environment.

But for the time being, there is only one show in town, and local authorities need to get what they can out of it.

Staff and councillors need to understand the new institutions. They need know that RDAs will be business led, regional chambers local authority led. They need to know what the different institutions will do: for example that RDAs will take over the Single

Regeneration Budget as well as the work of English Partnerships and the regional inward investment agencies; that chambers will be advisory and have their major impact on regional strategies; that the government will continue to rank and sign off European projects; that TECs and further education colleges will continue much as they are for the time being; that the Local Government Association will continue as the representative body for English local authorities.

The West Midlands experience suggest two particular emphases. The first concerns the Government Offices. These will continue to exist, and their regional directors will still have the opportunities to bring together local programmes of different Whitehall departments, and to channel money into partnerships. The RDAs will be important in some areas of work, but the Government Office role is potentially all embracing.

The second conclusion for the West Midlands is that the regional arms of the Local Government Association have huge potential. They are the bodies where all local authorities are represented, where counties can talk to districts, where sectoral committees can discuss and adopt strategies for their regions. They have the potential to develop into parliaments or assemblies for their regions.

I would like to acknowledge constructive comments from Sandy Taylor. The views here are mine, not those of Birmingham City Council.

The English Regions and the Wider Constitutional and Administrative Reforms

John Mawson,
Professor at the Aston Business School, University of Aston

New Labour's devolution policies are leading to a fundamental reshaping of UK territorial politics and administration. This section considers the changing relationships between various parts of the UK, between Whitehall and the English regions, and some of the implications for local authorities of the emerging governance structures.

It is clear that the economic, political and administrative forces that lead to the return of the regional and devolution agenda are deep-seated and their persistence may well lead to pressures for further changes. In this dynamic, the English regions are in a pivotal and evolving situation. The failure of the Callaghan administration to fully recognise concerns about the impact of devolution on the North East and other parts of England led to parliamentary opposition, the wrecking of the Devolution Bill and ultimately set in train events leading to the fall of the government in 1979. This time around it is important that as the devolution project unfolds it is viewed in its totality, taking into account the complex interactions between different parts of the UK. In this connection it is instructive to reflect on how the government's constitutional reform agenda may be viewed from an English perspective at the turn of the millennium.

SEVEN

Devolution – an English perspective

By the year 2000 the English regions will be surrounded by a range of new democratic structures and will inevitably be comparing their merits with arrangements for chambers and RDAs. In Scotland the parliament will take over Scottish Office functions and will have the ability to shape domestic policy and pursue primary legislation outside reserved areas. It will have a powerful political voice to articulate Scotland's interests in the economic and European spheres and the means to execute policy through a cohesive economic development network. This will be orchestrated through Scottish Enterprise and its network of Local Enterprise Companies in which local government is likely to be far more directly involved than has been the case to date. The Scottish parliament will offer local government the opportunity of a partnership role in shaping national legislation through various policy forums and will have the opportunity to reorganise, scrutinise and democratise the quangos, thereby opening this important area of the public domain to local democratic engagement.

Similar advantages will be available to the Northern Ireland Assembly in relation to the Northern Ireland Office, the ability to pass primary legislation in the domestic sphere and the inheritance of an economic development infrastructure boosted by substantial international funding and encouragement to inward investment. There will also be a strong momentum behind cross border links with the Republic in economic development, planning and transportation, with European Union support. The return of genuine sub-national democracy will present major challenges and opportunities for local authorities. While the National Assembly for Wales will inherit the Welsh Office, it will not have primary legislative capacity, but nevertheless will be able to exercise considerable powers over Welsh affairs including local government through secondary legislation. The Assembly will not have direct responsibility for the Welsh Development Agency which will remain a central government quango. Nevertheless there will be a strong steer from the Assembly over economic development policies and Wales will benefit from a restructured and strengthened body which will be regionalised and incorporate the business support/TEC network. The National Assembly for Wales itself will have regional committees to oversee its work throughout the country and this together with a powerful policy partnership will present local government with a major opportunity to influence and shape the emerging domestic agenda.

In the case of London, local authorities elsewhere in England will view with interest the work of the Mayor and Greater London Assembly which will inherit funding earmarked for the key services of police, fire and transport as well as responsibilities for strategic planning and economic development. The Mayor will have a powerful elected mandate to devise a unique form of strategic and land-use plan for the capital, provide a leadership and co-ordination role for the public sector and work in partnership with private and voluntary sectors towards agreed London-wide agendas. Unlike the situation elsewhere in England, the London Development Agency will be accountable directly to the Mayor and Assembly.

Finally, across the UK as a whole, the government is committed to the establishment of a Council of the Isles to address cross-border and strategic territorial issues such as those concerned with economic development, planning, transport and European funding and policies such as INTERREG, and Trans-European Networks, European Spatial Development. As the position currently stands it appears that three of the four territorial components of the UK: Scotland, Wales and Northern Ireland will be represented by devolved elected bodies while the fourth, the English regions, will have no equivalent political voice other than that representation through central government.

Territorial comparisons and momentum for further change

Taken together the various forms of devolution and the associated powers and responsibilities set out above may lead to unfavourable comparisons with what is on offer to the English regions. Elected politicians, business leaders, representatives of key regional institutions and other regional stakeholders such as trade unions, the voluntary and community sectors may take the view that their regions lack the necessary clout to articulate their interests, and that the RDAs do not possess sufficient powers and resources to be an effective counterweight. There may be concerns in border regions such as the North East about a 'shadow effect' from powerful neighbours with a perceived advantage in attracting inward investment or European funding. English local authorities may also view with envy the greater influence their counterparts are able to exercise over the newly elected assemblies and the opportunities which new legislation or the exercise of secondary legislation may provide.

Resentments at the regional level may be fuelled by the inbuilt financial advantage which Scotland and Wales secure from the so-called Barnett formula which determines the distribution of public expenditure between the separate parts of the UK. (Scotland currently receives £25 per capita more public expenditure per annum than the English regions, and Wales £15 more) Already the leading candidates for the position of elected Mayor in London have raised the issue, and the matter has recently been the subject of a Treasury Select Committee inquiry in which members from the north of England and London were vociferous in their complaints about the unfairness of the system. The previous Chief Secretary to the Treasury, Alastair Darling MP, indicated that there would be no review of the formula this side of the next election but others with a regional interest may not wish to let the matter rest. Indeed more widely, it seems likely that those aspects of public policy which have an explicit territorial dimension may well be subject to increasing public scrutiny not least because the new elected assemblies will see such matters as being at the heart of their concerns.

To take one example, the processes of demarcating assisted-area boundaries and determining eligibility criteria for national and European funding which historically were negotiated and resolved behind closed doors by senior officials and ministers in Whitehall and Brussels, will now be subject to far greater openness and transparency. The hidden geographical trade-offs between different parts of the UK which were made in the past to secure the greater national interest will now be exposed, making the resolution of these matters far more difficult from both an administrative and political point of view. While guidelines have been established about how such matters will be dealt with and the primacy of a single UK government position in Brussels has been emphasised, nevertheless, the stages leading up to an agreed position will prove far more difficult to handle. Similarly in the case of inward investment policy, the UK government has been working on a concordat between the various development agencies to ensure a more coherent national approach and to avoid wasteful competition in the post devolution era. However, the recent complaints from the North East business community about poaching of inward investment projects by Scottish Enterprise, albeit unfounded, suggests how difficult this task may prove to be in a climate of enhanced territorial competition.

In formal political terms feelings of comparative disadvantage are likely to be increasingly articulated through concerns about the so-called 'West Lothian question'. This was originally posed by Tam Dalyell MP at the time of the previous devolution debate when he highlighted the anomalous situation that Scottish MPs would have the right to vote on English affairs but that the equivalent right would not be available to English MPs. Conscious of these concerns the prime minister has already indicated that there will need to be some reduction in the number of Scottish MPs in due course but doubtless this will not be the end of it. The continuing roles of the Secretaries of State for Scotland and Wales (if not Northern Ireland), are likely to be questioned and there will be increasing calls to tackle the democratic deficit for England as a whole. Some have suggested a Select or Grand Committee for English Affairs while the Conservative Party is increasingly favouring the creation of an English parliament. The reform of the House of Lords presents a further opportunity to tackle the issue through the introduction of a regional dimension in an elected second chamber. While all these proposals are designed to introduce an explicitly English dimension into this new context there will be those from the regions who will be sceptical as to how far such structures will seriously challenge the centralising tendencies of London and the South East unless they are paralleled by elected regional assemblies.

Looking forward, then, the jury is out as to how far New Labour's present trajectory for the English regions will be able to absorb these various territorial pressures. The present commitment to consider further democratic and administrative reforms after the next election may or may not prove sufficient. The danger is that in the absence of a clearer way forward in the mean time, resentment may be channelled into an assault on the existing devolution reforms and set one part of the UK off against another in a series of acrimonious political and policy disputes.

The Prescott-Caborn axis has been a powerful voice in government for a democratic decentralisation agenda to the English regions. And without their forceful pursuit of the issue it is likely that even less might have been achieved, given the lack of interest elsewhere in the cabinet. However, while recognising the absence of a demand for elected regional government throughout England, it is possible to argue that more could have been done to address the perceived democratic deficit in the short term. The indirectly nominated chambers, for example, could have been given clearer roles in scrutiny, oversight and policy engagement with the RDAs, Government Offices and other dimensions of the public sector in the regions.

Notwithstanding these weaknesses, the onus is now on local government and other regional stakeholders to play their part in making sure that the new governance structures do work. Central government has offered the prospect of a greater level of involvement in regional decision-making through the chamber-RDA framework and the opportunity for further progress in the event of the build up of effective regional working and calls for a more formal political representation. Prescott and Caborn are acutely aware of the need for early success in the work of the RDAs and associated regional partnerships in order to convince sceptical cabinet colleagues of the case for further strengthening the emerging regional infrastructure in England

Whitehall, Devolution and the Regions

The arguments above have sought to highlight some of the possible difficulties which lie ahead if central government fails to view the devolution project in its totality. In the light of these concerns the article turns to consider some possible steps which could be taken in Whitehall to respond to these challenges and then goes on to explore in more detail central government's relationship with the regions and the challenges which the new governance structures present for local authorities.

Since coming to office, the prime minister has been keen to tackle the problem of departmentalism which is endemic in the civil service and presents particular problems for those concerned with the territorial management of public policy. Historically, block funding to the Scottish, Welsh and Northern Ireland Offices and the drawing together of domestic policy responsibilities under a single cabinet minister meant that the issue has been less of a problem in these countries than is the case in England. It was not until 1994 when John Major's government established the Government Offices for the Regions (drawing together environment, transport, education, employment and industry functions under a single senior civil servant) that there was an identifiable and cohesive central government presence in the English regions. Even then, key departments such as agriculture were not located within the GORs and there was no direct line management relationship with Executive Agencies and statutory agencies such as the Housing Corporation.

Co-ordination of the GOR roles at the centre through a Government Office management board (comprising senior officials from the GORs parent departments) has tended to focus on routine administrative matters, rather than on cross-cutting policy concerns (exceptions being competitiveness, regeneration and sustainability) and there have been limited connections with the processes of cabinet decision-making. Annually the GORs have submitted operational plans as part of the public expenditure planning process but the integration achieved regionally is not taken forward easily at the centre since the parent departments negotiate their GOR elements separately with the Treasury. These weaknesses are compounded by the fact that the Treasury itself does not engage in any detailed disaggregation or analysis of the distribution of public expenditure between or within regions.

There are signs that the prime minister's concerns about joined-up government are beginning to highlight these weaknesses at the centre through, for example, the Social Exclusion Unit's work on neighbourhood renewal and the Cabinet Office's recently announced review of 'government presence in cities and regions.' However, it remains to be seen how far these concerns about the need for a territorial perspective will be taken forward into the day-to-day workings of the machinery of government. At a time when the government is engaging in such a fundamental reshaping of the geography of British politics and public administration it is surprising that there appears to be so little strategic thinking in government about the implications. The closest to this is the Cabinet Committee chaired by the Lord Chancellor which is overseeing constitutional reforms. However, its remit is focusing on legal and constitutional matters rather than on the political and policy consequences of devolution.

Against this background and the apparent weaknesses in the present machinery of government the following steps could be considered in taking forward the devolution agenda.

- The development of a more explicit territorial perspective in the work of all relevant Whitehall departments, Executive Agencies and quangos, led by the Cabinet Office.
- The development of a far greater capacity to analyse the distribution of public expenditure between and within regions. Given the tensions that are bound to arise over public expenditure distribution the government could consider developing a regional 'needs-assessment process' linked to the longer term public expenditure planning.
- The development of a more strategic oversight over the evolving constitutional agenda and the reshaping of the geography of public policy. The government could consider establishing a powerful 'cross-cutting' cabinet committee to cover the nations/regions chaired by a senior government minister such

as the deputy prime minister.

- Each region/nation represented by a minister.
- Government 'beefing up' the Whitehall interface with the English regions by, for example, setting up a more strategic GOR management board which would report directly to the 'cross-cutting' cabinet committee.

Government Office for the Regions

In the debates about the emerging regional structures, the role of the Government Offices has yet to be fully considered. At the regional level, the key focus to date has been on the transfer of GOR staff and functions to the RDA, and the establishment of the new offices for the RDA boards. In most cases staff concerned will come from the SRB sections of Government Offices and from the DTI sections involved in inward investment, and possibly some dealing with innovation and technology transfer.

This transfer of staff should help to cement good working relationships and facilitate access to central government departments. Indeed, the GOR is a key fulcrum in the new governance structures. It is the obvious vehicle to facilitate collaboration between RDAs, chambers and regional stakeholders. It provides a clear single voice of Whitehall in the regions and if given the necessary support at the centre should help to avoid too many crossed wires. It could help to ensure that government departments, Executive Agencies and quangos not present in the GOR positively engage in the work of the RDAs and chambers. This will be essential if the RDAs are going to oversee an economic agenda which includes the work of TECs, Business Links and Regional Selective Assistance, the social economy, rural development, and related concerns in areas such as planning, transport and the environment. The GORs contribution will also be vital in ensuring the chambers are able to fulfill their role of commenting on the RDA's corporate plan and working with other regional partners in developing integrated regional strategies covering for example, transport, planning, environment, health education and economic policy. Without the Government Office facilitating these links it will be difficult to deliver the 'joined up' approach to regional development. Built into the remit of both the RDAs and chambers are certain ambiguities over roles and responsibilities which could lead to tensions or conflict if not handled sensitively. The RDA, for example, while required to take account of the views of the chamber does not necessarily have to take its observations on board. Moreover it has the right to consult regional stakeholders and partnerships directly thus enabling it to play off one group of actors against another. In the short term at least there may be a need for the GOR to help private-sector-led RDA boards understand and come to terms with some of the trade offs that are necessary in the complex interface between public and private worlds.

If the GORs are to successfully fulfill this pivotal role at the regional level then ministers will need to get the message across in Whitehall about the need to co-operate in their activities. It will also require ensuring that they have a clear and powerful entry point into the Whitehall machinery of government, perhaps through a strengthened Government Office management board, as suggested previously. Equally, however, there remains the danger that the Government Office officials could end up exercising far too much power and influence in the new structures if regional stakeholders do not rise to the challenge and opportunities offered by the new RDA chamber framework. In the end a more locally accountable and transparent policy framework can only be achieved by the active participation of local authorities and other regional stakeholders.

Local Authorities

In this new institutional context local authorities face a series of challenges and opportunities as the new working relationships unfold. If they are to work effectively in this new sphere of public policy, they will need to ensure that they speak with a single voice and that the emerging regional Local Government Association and English Regional Association structures service their chambers effectively.

Undoubtedly there is the danger that the new regional institutions will seek to take over roles and responsibilities better left to local authorities. Whether RDAs and chambers add value to – or end up competing with and duplicating – existing local government functions will in part depend on the quality of partnership relationships and the need to reach agreement among partners as to the best division of labour in a particular policy area.

At the moment local authorities are struggling to get to grips with the new governance structures. In order to do so, many – particularly smaller authorities – will need to develop new competences (such as understanding European structural funds, how to develop new forms of regional strategy) and new organisational capacity (such as the servicing of members on the RDA board, the development of communication and accountability structures between chambers RDAs, LGAs, and so on). All this will require extra time on the part of officers and members and will involve additional resource costs. In this context it is instructive to consider the various pressures placed on a typical district or unitary in, say Essex. In the emerging situation it will be asked to participate in, and fund a wide array of organisations including South East Region Planning Conference, the South East Regional Forum, the Eastern Region Conference, the emerging East of England Chamber, the Essex Economic Partnership, the RDO for the Eastern Region – the East of England Investment Agency, the Local Business Link, the Essex TEC, the LGA electoral college for Herts, Beds, Essex, and so on. This comes on top of a modernising local government agenda where new local structures and partnerships have to be forged. In this complex new world of regional governance there is clearly the danger that authorities could be played off against one other by the various regional players and central government departments.

However, if local authorities learn to work together at the regional level and cope with these problems then there will be significant opportunities. They will have a chance to have a greater engagement in, and influence upon central government decision-making by giving a steer to the strategic priorities and work of RDAs and GORs, through the regional chamber. By showing that devolution works, they may in due course be able to secure increased powers and responsibilities and benefit from improved central/local relationships. In the past there have been significant areas of public policy – for example, DTI functions and health – which have operated independently of local authorities. Now for the first time there is an opportunity to be involved in these policy areas through the regional chambers and their relationship with GORs.

The challenge to local government is to influence the form and nature of the structures as they evolve. Officers from local government will need to be involved in setting up the offices for the RDAs, in liaising with the GORs, in establishing support structures for RDA members and the new chambers and in facilitating the accountability links both to local partnerships and between the different regional administrative structures. Members will need to work with the new devolved democratic and regional structures to secure more cohesive joined up government and the development of regional strategies in partnership with leaders of the business community, voluntary and community sectors, trades unions, higher education, and so on. It will be important to work through the national and regional local government associations to build alliances across the country to ensure the interests of local government are properly represented and to avoid the worst excesses of 'dog-eat-dog' area chauvinism. The national local government associations and bodies such as the English Regional Association will need to work together and take positions on some of the UK wide territorial policy issues highlighted in the first part of this paper. Whilst acknowledging that on occasions there will be legitimate differences of interest over for example assisted area status, there will be many situations where a powerful local government voice will be important in discussions with central government and the European Union.

Crucially, in playing a leading role in the newly established chambers local authorities will need to help develop the capability of other key stakeholders to engage in dialogue, policy formation and implementation – especially the voluntary and community sector. Voluntary sector regional support networks have begun to emerge in all the regions to provide technical support and articulate a sector view. However, they are chronically under-funded and there is responsibility on central government to do far more in this connection. At the end of the day, these new tasks will place a considerable burden on an already stretched local authority sector and it is not unreasonable that they should expect some support from central government if they are to play a leading role in developing and servicing the new governance structures. Central government is providing a significant level of taxpayers money to set up and run the new democratic forums elsewhere in the UK. There is no logical reason why it should not do the same for the English regions.

RECOMMENDATIONS

It is recommended that local authorities lobby for a strategic, cohesive approach to constitutional reform involving:

- an explicit territorial perspective across Whitehall with active participation of all relevant departments, Executive Agencies and quangos in the new regional structures
- the development of new Whitehall and Cabinet structures to ensure a clear overview of the evolving constitutional reforms which recognises the consequences for public policy nationally and regionally
- Whitehall recognition of the pivotal role of GORs in facilitating the new regional structures and drawing together the various dimensions of the public sector
- a clear and powerful entry point for GORs into the Whitehall machinery of government.

It is recommended that local authorities rise to the challenge of the new regional structures by:

- giving them sufficient priority to ensure that the regional structures are successfully launched, but at the same time pressing for significant central government backing to resource these new roles

- taking the opportunity to influence the form and nature of the new structures to ensure that the local democratic view is forcefully present
- working with the new devolved democratic and regional structures to secure more cohesive 'joined up' government
- building alliances across the nations and regions to avoid area chauvinism
- facilitating the capability of local stakeholders, particularly the local community, to engage in dialogue and policy formation on these strategic issues while at the same time pressing for central government support for capacity building.

From Regional Development to Regional Devolution

Alan Whitehead MP

With the appointment of chairs and members of the English Regional Development Agencies, the reality of economic regionalism is at last upon us. To those who long carried the flame of regional devolution when it seemed that there were only a few guttering candles in the dark, that the RDAs are there at all is a small miracle: to those who have come to the debate later, and who have less emotional baggage to consider, they represent a strange starting point for any thoroughgoing regional devolution. They are, indeed, animals far removed from the democratic bodies of regional governance found elsewhere in Europe.

The case for regional devolution

It is beyond dispute that the existence of the RDAs owes much to the persistence of John Prescott and Richard Caborn in pursuing an idea that they were convinced was vital for the regeneration and rebalancing of Britain's regional economy: and, indeed, soon for the first time there will be agencies that genuinely represent an agenda other than that of the centre. The weakness of the current position is that, arguably, one would not have started with RDAs had other options been available, and that the powers they have are largely restricted to those in the gift of the Department of Environment, Transport, and the Regions to bestow. The boundaries, furthermore, remain those of the Government Offices for the Regions, developed as a limited administrative devolution with no organic sense of what a region is.

The new RDAs, therefore, face discontent on several fronts and from quite disparate groups. Dedicated 'regionalists' express distrust of the government's future devolution agenda and attack them for being faint echoes of the cherished regional government of past campaigns. Many in local government (particularly at county level) consider that RDAs represent a Trojan horse, marking out the starting point of a journey that will lead inexorably to the removal of powers from local government to regions which they believe will be little more than post boxes for the centre anyway. The barricades go up around 'localism' as a counter to these new developments. There are also, of course, some who believe that all this devolution business was a big mistake, and consider that successful opposition to RDAs will somehow start to unwind all the nasty business in Scotland, Wales and London.

We can safely discount the credibility of the first and last positions. On the matter of the first, anyone who is serious about regionalism knows that to succeed, a trajectory has to be established. It always was improbable that full blown regional government would suddenly appear, and even if it did it would fail to implant itself because the public remains sceptical of the merits of full English devolution. The debate will only be won by long dialogue and patient example, not by sudden constitutional coups. The reactionary position of opposing all developments presents an incredible proposition of all the work on Scottish, Welsh and London government being wound back: a belief now no longer shared by most Conservatives who are planning to participate in the elections shortly to be held for all three bodies.

The strategy set out here assumes that local government benefits from regional devolution: many of those in local government wary of RDAs are perhaps looking at their fears of what happens if it all goes wrong, rather than the gains if it goes right. The conundrum of all this is that local government attitudes towards RDAs and the subsequent process of democratisation could make devolution work or fail: putting the positive case is therefore an important starting point.

There will undoubtedly be some perceived losers from the process: some county councils that consider themselves as, in essence, regional strategic authorities will have a rude awakening.

Other than that, the establishment of a democratically elected, strategic tier of government away from the centre would crystallise and entrench a definition of the role of the centre, the regional and the local. At present, regional governance is an uncertain morass of central directive through quangos and agencies, tentative regional planning through indirectly accountable bodies, and an imprecise engagement with some regional and sub regional issues through the larger counties. A clearly constituted regional body with a democratic mandate will overwhelmingly make a case for the accretion of powers from the GORs, from regional quangos and from direct government control. This will, therefore, define what is indisputably 'the local'. A successful regional tier will strengthen local government by giving it clear territory within which to work: and the possibility of this territory being attacked, as occurred during the 1980s, will be very difficult thereafter to envisage. The economic and political function of local government will therefore be guaranteed by the constitutional settlement that will follow successful devolution.

The difficulty many encounter in taking these logical steps arises in large measure because of a serious and long-apparent division in Labour party thinking on regionalism: namely that there are 'constitutional' issues and 'economic' issues, and that it is quite proper and manageable to keep the two apart. Before the election, this resulted in the Millan Commission (Regional Policy Commission, 1996) producing proposals on 'economic' regionalism, whilst at the same time Jack Straw produced an entirely different set of regional 'constitutional' ideas with the document *A Choice for England* (Labour party, 1995).

In reality the two approaches cannot be separated, or at least, not over a long period without some glaring problems arising. The RDAs, for example, can only be defended from the charge that they are to become a series of regional 'super-quangos' if we make the assumption that the boards represent part of a process rather than the end point. Otherwise, in addition to the 'quango' charge, the government will have laid long term regional policy and the European dimension it represents largely in the hands of the private sector, which will, to say the least, jar with the structures commonly in place in other EU states. In this scenario, RDAs will not be viewed much more favourably for collaborative purposes than are the Government Offices currently.

If we assume that the creation of RDAs is, or ought to be, part of a process, then how can we keep an agenda of decentralisation and devolution on course taking the reality of RDAs into account? The accepted wisdom is that any further moves towards regional democratic government in the UK will take place well the other side of the next election, and even then only in the context of referenda and (at least, according to Jack Straw) not without unitary local government. Some have viewed these constraints as, to all intents and purposes, placing further developments off the agenda. This is, in my view a premature and pessimistic assumption to make.

The key point is that RDAs are there, and can, by successfully operating, demonstrate the wisdom of making further progress towards effective and democratic regionalisation. The *sine qua non* of any further progress, therefore, is that RDAs as they stand now, within current boundaries, are perceived to work well. A boycott or a grudging approach to RDAs by local authorities and other local bodies because they do not represent 'real' regions will simply fuel the arguments of the opponents of any form of decentralisation that there is 'no demand' for regionalisation, and that any experiment is doomed to failure.

Moving regional policy forward

Working from this imperative, there are a number of promising avenues for moving the process forward.

First, there is the continued, and public recognition of intention to go further, at least by John Prescott and Richard Caborn. The White Paper preceding the legislation stated that: "The government is committed to move to directly-elected regional government in England where there is a demand for it, alongside devolution in Scotland and Wales and the creation of the Greater London Authority."

Richard Caborn confirmed this when he stated in a Parliamentary Answer in February 1998 that: "[the RDAs] will consult the chambers that are being set up in the English regions, and in the fullness of time we shall give the people of the regions through a referendum or other such mechanism the opportunity to state whether they want a directly elected regional assembly."

Second, there is the early operation of the regional chambers. Their existence is an important bridge – and a development that would not have taken place had there been no intention to at least countenance further forms of devolution. There is, however, a great responsibility on the shoulders of the chambers. While they should be conscious of their roles as 'assemblies in waiting', an overweening attitude or a series of confrontations with the RDAs will jeopardise the success of the whole enterprise, since they will allow themselves to be portrayed as 'power mad' at a time when it will be impossible to counter such a claim by constructive action. Leaders of the chambers should act to demonstrate that they are potentially able to exercise regional power democratically, rather than make the mistake of assuming that the very indirect mandate that they presently have is democracy already arrived.

Third, the development of the Scottish parliament and the Welsh and London assemblies will be taking place in parallel with the early operation of the RDAs. Each one, will in different ways, have a relationship with economic development functions that will underline possible ways of integrating the role of RDAs with democratic structures. However, the exact relationship differs in each case, and it is worth briefly noting what they are. The Scottish parliament will have a quasi-national relationship with the Scottish Development Agency, and in many ways will represent a arrangement beyond that which even a fully democratic regional assembly would go. The National Assembly for Wales will, it seems, have no direct relationship with the reformed Welsh Development Agency, which according to schedule 9 of the Act will be reformed from the existing WDA and the Welsh Land Agency, entirely subject to ministerial discretion. This undoubtedly reflects the sorry history of the Agency, and should not be taken as any sort of 'test bed' for English regional arrangements.

London, however, presents a very different case. Despite the 'local government' feel of a number of pronouncements about London, and the obvious 'local' sound of the London Mayor, the legislation on London clearly casts the assembly as a regional body in all but name. The GLA will, therefore, assume the functions of the LDA in the same way as one might envisage for eventual regional assemblies, but on a much faster time scale. In London, unlike Wales, there will also be a direct line of account from agency to authority. The template to watch is London, and the extent to which political progress on assemblies is made with trepidation or confidence hinges on the success of the GLA/LDA relationship.

What London will not give guidance on, though, is the process by which regional chambers might become legitimated. In the case of London, a simple referendum on present (and well established) boundaries sufficed. There are problems in the regions, however: what is meant by 'where a demand exists'? And does the process of legitimation necessarily have to be by a referendum? The successful establishment of democratically accountable regional assemblies in Spain perhaps points the way. The process there was flexible: the *prima facie* establishment of regions was tested by, among other things, the agreement on boundaries among municipalities: and the tests of legitimacy included cumulative motions of assent by local bodies. In an atmosphere generally conducive to an assembly such as may well exist in the North and possibly the West Midlands, the active involvement and consent of most of the local authorities in the region would allow for a more satisfactory method of opinion-sounding since a campaign could be fought authority-by-authority, rather than by a single winner-takes-all poll.

However, after all this there remains an inescapable logical bottom line: there must be provision for chambers to precipitate a referendum or similar legitimation process on boundaries other than those that exist currently. Only in a few regions do boundaries satisfactorily reflect organic regions, and it is on the cards that some referenda could be lost not because people do not want regionalism but because they do not want the region they are offered. The likelihood of success in the South East or the South West, for example, must be seen as low by this criterion. Alternatively, some chambers may decide not to press ahead for this reason, and we will have the curious outcome of a three-tier regional system. Some regions will be democratic and 'legitimate', some will be ossified into arms-length democracy, while others will be 'failed' regions, having lost referenda and condemned to drift with clearly discredited chambers. The Spanish experience suggests that the 'me too' feeling is strong, once regionalism is seen to be a forceful tide. To trip up because no mechanism exists for the agreed evolution of unwieldy RDAs and chambers into more meaningful and locally intelligible bodies would be unforgivable.

RECOMMENDATIONS

The main purpose of this section has been to set out a route by which the goal of regional devolution can be approached from the starting point of the present reality of RDAs. In doing that, the overwhelming advantage to local government of defined spheres of competence between the centre, the regions and the local has been emphasised. The recommendations for the success of that route can be summarised as:

- RDAs must be seen to work as they stand, and local government should ensure that they are supported
- Regional chambers should pay careful regard to their relationships with RDAs in the period prior to any move towards elected regional chambers
- The development of the relationship between the Greater London Authority and the London Development Agency should be closely monitored as a possible paradigm of future chamber/RDA relations
- Local government should consider whether it wishes to endorse a test of legitimation for regional assemblies by way of a rolling endorsement by local authorities, rather than a one-off referendum
- Local government should press for mechanisms to be in place, providing for the formation of regional assemblies on boundaries other than those of the Government Offices for the Regions.

References

ALG, *Advancing Together, Regional Assembly for Yorkshire and Humberside,* (London, Association of London Government, 1998)

H J Bennett and R Patel, *Sustainable Regeneration Strategies,* Local Economy Vol 10 No. 2 pages 133-148 (London, 1995)

The Constitution Unit, *Regional Government in England* (London, 1996)

Commission of the European Communities, *Growth, Competitiveness and Employment,* European Union White Paper (Brussels, 1993)

Commission of the European Communities, *Agenda 2000* (Brussels, 1997)

Commission of the European Communities, *Draft Structural Fund Regulations* (Brussels, 1998)

COSLA, *Preparing new SPDs* (Edinburgh, 1998)

DfEE, *TECs: Meeting the Challenge of the Millennium* [Consultation Paper] (London, DfEE Publications, 1998)

DETR, *Response to Department of Trade and Industry, Competitiveness: Forging Ahead* [White Paper] (London, The Stationery Office, 1995)

DETR, *Building Partnerships for Prosperity* [White Paper] (London, 1997a)

DETR, *Regeneration Programmes, the way forward,* Discussion Paper (1997b)

DETR, *A New Deal for Transport: Better for everyone* [White Paper on Integrated Transport] (London, The Stationery Office, 1998)

DoH, *Our Healthier Nation* (London, Stationery Office, 1998) Cm 3852

DTI, *Helping Businesses to Win* (London, Stationery Office, 1994)

DTI, *Competitiveness: Forging Ahead* [White Paper] (London, Stationery Office, 1995)

M Dorsmen, 'Reviewing the Role of TECs: Will they meet the Challenge?', in Local Work (no. 7), (Manchester, CLES, August 1998)

J Dungey, *Mapping the Future* (London, LGIU, 1997)

J H Dunning, E Bannerman, S M Lundan (with a statement by the Economic Council), *Competitiveness and Industrial Policy in Northern Ireland,* Northern Ireland Economic Development Office Research Monograph 5 (1998)

Environment, Transport and Regional Affairs Select Committee: 1st Report (12 January 1998); 2nd Special Report (18 March 1998)

Environment, Transport and Regional Affairs Committee, *Regional Development Agencies* (The Stationery Office, 1998) Cm 3814

S F Fothergill, *Labour's Regional Policy Commission: An Assessment of its Proposals*, Discussion Paper (London, Regional Studies Association, 1997)

A Harding, R Evans, M Parkinson, P Garside, *Regional Government in Britain* (Bristol, Policy Press, 1996)

B W Hogwood, *Mapping the regions: Boundaries, co-ordination and government* (Bristol, The Policy Press, 1996)

S Holland, *New Dimensions to European Finance* (London, LGIU, 1998)

W Hutton, *The State We're In,* (London, Jonathan Cape, 1995)

The Labour party, *A choice for England* (London, Labour party, 1995)

The Local Futures Group, *The London Study. A Strategic Framework for London* (London, 1998)

The Local Government Association, *New Commitment to Regeneration: Briefing and Guidance* (London, LGA, 1998)

S Marvin, S Graham, S Guy, *Privatised Utilities and Regional Management* (Harlow, SEEDs, 1996)

P Murphy and R Caborn, *Regional Government for England – an Economic Imperative* (Sheffield Hallam University, 1995)

C Oppenheim (ed), *An Inclusive Society. Strategies for Tackling Poverty,* (London, IPPR,1998)

M O'Toole, *Regional Development Agencies and Europe* (European Information Service, Issue 186, January 1998)

J Plummer and T Zipfel, *The Role of TECs and LECs in Regeneration* (Bristol, Joseph Rowntree Foundation and the Policy Press, 1998)

Regional Policy Commission (Millan Commission), *Renewing the Regions: Strategies for Regional Economic Development* [Report of the Commission] (Sheffield Hallam University, 1996)

Regional Development Agencies Act (London, Stationery Office, 1998)

R Reich, *The Work of Nations* (New York, Simon and Schuster, 1991)

SEU, *Bringing Britain Together: a national strategy for neighbourhood renewal* (London, Stationery Office, 1998) Cm 4045

J Shutt and A Colwell, *Towards 2006* (London, LGIU, 1997)

S Tindale, *Devolution on Demand* (London, IPPR, 1995)

HM Treasury/DTI, *Innovating for the Future: Investing in R&D* (1998)

Further information about RDAs is available on the DETR website: www.open.gov.uk

About the contributors

Ines Newman is Co-ordinator of the South East Economic Development Strategy

Jo Dungey is a Policy Officer at the Local Government Information Unit

Michael Ward is Director of the Centre for Local Economic Strategies

Stuart Wilks-Heeg is Research Fellow at the European Institute for Urban Affairs at Liverpool John Moores University

Adrian Colwell is European and International Affairs Officer at the Convention of Scottish Local Authorities

Liz Kerry is Director of the Regional Assembly for Yorkshire and Humberside

Andrew Coulson is Senior Lecturer at the Institute for Local Government Studies, University of Birmingham, and an elected member of Birmingham City Council

John Mawson is Professor at the Aston Business School, University of Aston

Alan Whitehead is Member of Parliament for Southampton Test, and was a member of the Millan Commission.

All contributors have written for this publication in a personal capacity